CW01597771

THE POETRY GAMES

Voices Across England

Edited by Cheryl Whitfield

First published in Great Britain in 2014 by:

YoungWriters

Remus House
Coltsfoot Drive
Peterborough
PE2 9BF
Telephone: 01733 890066
Website: www.youngwriters.co.uk

Book Design by Ashley Janson

SB ISBN 978-1-78443-114-3

Printed and bound in the UK by BookPrintingUK
Website: www.bookprintinguk.com

Foreword

Since our inception in 1991, Young Writers has endeavoured to promote poetry and creative writing within schools by running annual nationwide competitions. These competitions are designed to develop and nurture the burgeoning creativity of the next generation, and give them valuable confidence in their own abilities.

For our latest competition The Poetry Games, young writers from across the country were given the challenge to stand up for what they believe in using nothing but the power of the pen. Using poetry as their tool, these aspiring poets were given the opportunity to express their thoughts and feelings on the topics that matter to them through verse.

Whilst skilfully conveying their opinions through poetry, the writers showcased in this collection have simultaneously managed to give poetry a breath of fresh air, brought it to life and made it relevant to them. Using a variety of themes and styles, our featured poets leave a lasting impression of their inner thoughts and feelings, making this anthology a rare insight into the next generation.

Contents

THE POEMS

Drama

Nothing is better than hiding behind a mask,
to put on different faces.
How adventurous are the characters,
experimenting with different emotions,
and exploring various personalities.
Paint yourself envious green,
or perhaps raging red.
The chemistry between the actors,
Is stronger than atomic bonds.
However shy you may be,
you'll always be a loser if you don't try
Failure is a part of success.
With a swoosh,
the curtains sweep across the stage,
and all the drama comes to an end.

Sharukaa Uthayasekaran (12)

Away For The Holidays - Haiku

An abandoned house -
Before, bustling with home life.

Alone once again.

Ellie Worthington (16)

Nelson Rolihlahla Mandela

A legend was born
Not just a man
July 18th 1918
So deep he swam.

Fought for human rights
Strove for South Africa's best
You never thought of giving up
Better than all the rest.

27 years went by
Because the oppressed wanted liberty
It wasn't right, it was wrong
South Africa was left in misery.

Set free in 1990
He heard the world's cry
Continued to fight for rights
But in our heart's, he'll never die.

His priority was never revenge
But some stumbled the wrong way
Inspiration, dedication, liberation
2013, Mandela passed away.

His life was brutal,
His life was hard
Although some let him down
His fans were always on guard.

You always told us,
To stand up high
And to never be burned down
But to finish with that proud goodbye.

Madiba, one of the greatest
Taught us all a lesson
To never ever give up
But to always count your blessings.

Narissa Alves (13)

Kraznir A World Of Wonder!

Kraznir 2000 years ago,
A time that I will always know
Where warriors roam and wizards trek
Where creatures at night don't rest their heads
Food and death is all they think
There for creating blood bath sinks

Swords and shields are their only friends
That will stay by their sides till the end
Tiptoe scamper against the walls
As they watch their mortal enemies fall

But there is a good side to this world
A better side for us to unfold
A place less slippery and slimy as Kraznir
A place called Slinsil where all is well
Where there is peace and mystical magic spells
But Kraznir and Slinsil are at great war.

Cataclysmic fights as vicious as boars
Will Kraznir's icy hearts begin to thaw
Or will they just freeze more
Will this war end well or will it be the last they tell?

We all feel like this sometimes
But don't worry it's not a crime
Against friends and families we really do love
But on the inside we do act tough.

Bradley Wilson (13)

A Creative Poem

The blue light was as bright as the sun
As the flittering fairies flow by
They said it was a big one
When the angels had come, the blue light appeared dum!

The forests stood by
In the hollow bright light
A big hole appeared
A yellow one, with hairs on the branches
This was an adventure to eternity

Hundreds of apples
Hundreds of apples
Stood by with sticks that have done tricks
Melting in toffee,
Sweet as honey
And heat to swell well

Apples are red
Apples are green
They are just like your daily routine

The forest has trees
When they cried,
The branches had come out of their eyes.

Pavithran Pakkiyaeeswaran

Society

All you can see is the girl with eyes of joy,
What you can't see is a girl crying through her nights.
All you can see is the girl with no fears,
What you can't see is a girl, her knees weak with dread.
All you see is the girl, picture of innocence,
What you can't see is a girl, scars lacing her arms.
All you can see is the girl full of life,
What you can't see is a girl with pain killing her.
All you can see is the girl with a bright smile,
What you can't see is a girl screaming with silent anger.
All you can see is the girl with goals and a future,
What you can't see is a girl lost in despair.
All you can see is the girl with a personality on fire,
What you can't see is a girl frozen with sorrow and guilt.
All you can see is the girl with the image,
What you can't see is her mistakes and regret.
All you can see is my personal disguise,
What you can't see is the truth hidden from my lies.

Millie (14)

Who Am I?

Who am I?
I am unwanted, forgotten
I am the unheard cries and whines
I am the heartbroken, the hurt and sad
I am lost and lonely with that special one
I am waiting to have a home to call mine
I am waiting for you.

I am the one whose tail wags and my motor purrs when I see you
I am hoping to be accepted into your warm embrace
I am the one you choose to save
I am the one who will be there to welcome you home with a big smile.

So once again, who am I?
I am your new friend
I am the one you adopted which I am forever grateful
I am the one who will curl up beside you when you need comforting
I am the one who will have a head to lend for you to pet when you need this soothing.
I am the one that will never leave you and will always be by your side
I am the one that doesn't care how you look or care what you do,
because I will always love you.
So one last time, who am I?
I am your cat
I am your dog
I am the one
So let me be yours and please from the top to the bottom of my heart adopt me.
Let me love you
Let me call your home mine
Let me be there for you.

Layla Bhatti (14)
Canons High School, Edgware

Hanging Above The Clouds

Bound by the shackles of petty justice,
I lay here anticipating my fate.
Slashed her throat swiftly with my lewd cutlass.
The hate inside me refuses to wait.

Yet every day, the lass who comes and sweeps,
Imprisoned for life seems carefree with she.
Enlightens my days here, though yet to meet.
The abyss of lust is not to be seen.

So then, we go. The balcony is ours.
Love overpowers the sense of escape.
Plucking the string of love with a guitar.
The courts disagree - they declared it rape.

My fate remains by a necklace of rope.
Hollering her name - the cause of death - hope.

Serena Kutty (14)
Guru Nanak Sikh Academy, Hayes

Life On The Line

War is putting your life on the line
Soldiers serving their time

People waving flags for their country
Families' hearts being destroyed, on the contrary

Many stayed strong
As they knew they weren't in the wrong

I lost my dad on the battlefield
I wish we all had a big shield

My mother died
I'm sick and tired
When's it all going to end?

Manjot Singh (11)
Guru Nanak Sikh Academy, Hayes

Streets Of London

Street of London,
Safe or not?
Free space for bullies.
As free as a bird.
Only the boys in blue.
Knives not tolerated,
but still used.
Mainly alcoholics,
at vile pubs.
Guns and teens don't mix,
but still do.
Victims found dead.
Coloured in blood-red.
Smokers ruin the atmosphere,
whilst drinking beer.
Drug dealers selling,
to the innocent.
Making money,
thinking it is funny.
Children in gangs:
graffitiing, vandalising,
robbing as well as stealing.
Eventually getting caught,
by the boys in blue.

Are the streets safe?
I say not.

Dilshaan Grewal (12)
Guru Nanak Sikh Academy, Hayes

Forgotten

Trying to forget the past,
but the memories still last.
All through the night,
she wakes up in fright.

Thinking there's nowhere to go,
no one cares enough to show,
although it was long ago;
people still, don't want to know.

Every day her light fades away,
with nothing wanting her to stay.
Even starting to convey,
what could be, quite grey.

No matter what they say,
no matter what they do,
all she does is pray,
hoping there's a way.

Maineen Khurana (16)
Guru Nanak Sikh Academy, Hayes

Good-For-Nothing Girl

Can't I be unique?
Like Rosa Parks who protested against racism?
Freedom flying like an eagle.
Out of reach for me.

Why can't I live my dreams?
At least nothing will be as it seems.
Why am I forced for everything?
Being treated unlike a king.

Left out and ostracised.
Not even educated and wised.
Life is mine, not yours, it's mine.
I'm totally not fine.

And I can't even call Childline.
I don't have water, so forget about wine.
All that's there is the wall staring at me.
Whilst tears drip to make a river, you see.

Drip! Drip! Drip!
There go my tears before a loud whip.
Yes, it was always me.
And it still will be.
Being treated worse than a tree.
Why am I in poverty?

Don't I have the right to live?
Why are all my dreams being shattered?
One to the other which leaves me speechless.

Why is everyone so mean?
I am a human being.
I have to bear those threats all day.
From hundreds and thousands of bullies.
Those gossips don't leave chances to humiliate me.

Why do I have to be me?
Why can't I go to school?
I'm not a living tool.
I'm not there to be used and thrown away.
I have feelings too.

I have no shelter to protect me from a storm.
Living in a train station isn't warm.
No one cares if I'm happy or sad.

Why can't I have a foster dad?
At least I won't be as mad.
And I won't feel as bad.

Why am I a miserable girl?
Aren't I as special as a pearl?
Why am I me?

Mandeep Sehdev (12)
Guru Nanak Sikh Academy, Hayes

Life

Life is a wonderful gift . . . Embrace it . . .
It starts with a new day by waking up,
Life is a challenge, come on complete it . . .
Full of opportunities use it . . . Don't waste it . . .

The life is a mystery, unfold it, solve it.
It states life in a way . . . We don't even know
Life is a goal . . . Achieve it.
Full of promise . . . Full fill it.

Life is tragedy . . . Face it, accept it.
Life is precious . . . Hold it, don't lose it.
Life is an adventure . . . Enjoy it . . . Explore it.
Life is love . . . Just love it.

This is how life is . . .

Hearts meet and separate . . .
Live it, live it, live it . . .

Muskan Kapoor (12)
Guru Nanak Sikh Academy, Hayes

Thy Has Died

Scarring the breaches of years
Wavering the trees of light
Navigating stars with dynamite
Roaring like encrypted bears elite
Flames evaporating into death,
for I have betrayed,
thy has died

Gradually devouring the meal,
licking the surface of tears
Growing like a versatile reptile,
no ice, no water,
can slow the emotion that is beginning to leer,
You'll just have to wait till it comes crashing into your ear,
for I have betrayed,
thy has died

The anger, the reception will all come into deception
The thought has now been caught,
for I have betrayed,
thy has died

It is too late, for the fire, the anger, to come crashing into me,
the breaching has stopped, the roaring has finished,
the wavering has come to an end,
for I have betrayed,
thy has died

Now the gods all agree of 'your' fake pedigree
Now Zeus and Saturn would have heard you proclaim,
but now it is too late,
'twas your death at stake,
now you are now on the ground,
for I have betrayed,
thy has died

On the way to Hell,
all the ways have been held
The whispers of the dead have spread,
for I have betrayed,
thy has died.

Simrandeep Kaur (12)
Guru Nanak Sikh Academy, Hayes

Birds

Pretty birds always flying in the sky,
The same old birds we all buy.
Very beautiful are their wings,
Sweet and softly, the way they sing.

Playing around every day,
Not a penny do they pay.
Cute and innocent are their eyes,
Their innocence never ever lies.

Delicate are their colourful wings,
They have pride and honour just like kings.
These birds fly and always tweet,
They never stop to have a seat.

Late night is the time they sleep,
And never ever do they weep.
They always look after their kids,
Their nests like upside-down lids.

Pawandeep Sehdev (13)
Guru Nanak Sikh Academy, Hayes

My Brave Brother

Oh, I really do miss him
He has to come back to look after him
I hope he's okay up there
It seems like some people just don't care
He's further away from me than the moon
I hope he will come back soon
Oh, I really do miss him
The light of my life has gone dim
My mum's now living like a bird set free
I just cannot believe it
I hope he rests in peace
Oh, I really do miss him

Esha Rudki (12)
Guru Nanak Sikh Academy, Hayes

A Father's Daughter

He takes a step, heart stops he's shot down,
Right atrium pierced, a dad falls to the ground.

Teddy bear, old hard-crusted to touch,
dead plastic eyes who've seen far too much.
A rip in the lining just over its heart,
a smile on its lips but it's just a facade.
In a box there it lays with toys that can sing,
three from the thumb, a cold tarnished ring.

A daughter comes running and digs out the box,
she screams and she shouts and she opens the lock.
A Barbie, a Ken with perfect blonde hair,
but she doesn't see them, her eyes on the bear.
She squeezes him, cradles him, throws him around,
A game! With no guns, where he can't touch the ground.

She stitches him nicely, wipes dust off his eyes,
she desperately dreams that the toy comes alive.
Her classmates cry for her, 'the teddy won't wake'.
but what if her friends, they made a mistake?
The teddy is up and he's free of his lock,
smiling and happy and out of his box.

Max Thomas (16)
Hampton School, Hampton

As Houses Fly

One day the flood gates opened
Not gradually
But quick and sharp
Letting thoughts gallop
Astride a wave of memories
Locked with emotions
Held fast by the guilt

You overflow and run
Not from you but from yourself
And you run till you can't stand so you sit
Till you can't think
And then they shut
And the world is right again
No colours
Or sounds or lights
Things are still
As the wind rips the branches from the leaves

Yet still there's a nagging
That itches on the inside
You can't quite get enough
Just a bit more
So you can see the air swim again
And watch
As houses fly.

Sam Millward (13)
Hampton School, Hampton

Black Or White

Black or white,
Pink or blue,
It doesn't matter what colour you are as long as you're you.

The moon is white,
The sun is yellow,
We are like toasted marshmallows.
Sweet inside,
Different colours,
Nice and safe under covers.
The trees are green,
The soil is brown,
The ground is hard,
The earth is round,
And we are in the middle,
We are bound.

Daniel Hayward (13)
Holy Family RC & CE College, Heywood

Poverty

In the streets cold I lie,
People passing by not a word they say,
These lonely days just pass on by,
No friends, no family just me, myself and I,
But one day my lonely cold days will be no more.

The money doesn't mean anything,
Just a home will do, when that day comes no longer I will be cold.
These people I see with big fur coats,
Just stare at me like I am nothing,
Without any hope I sit and beg . . .

Jodie Smith (12)
Holy Family RC & CE College, Heywood

Drawing

Swirls and swiggles
Zigzags and lines
My picture will give you the giggles
It is sure to blow your minds.

Red and yellow
Green and blue
It's not a marshmallow
And it's not your shoe.

It's tall and colourful
Grand and big
It's not thoughtful
But it's guarded by a giant purple pig.

Can you guess what it is?
I'm sure you can't.

It's a rainbow in the sky!
With unicorns and pigs!

Chloe Mather (11)
Holy Family RC & CE College, Heywood

The Snow Leopard

There was a snow leopard
Who got peppered
With a meal
This hunter was the real deal
One day it was in the snow
Next above the fireplace
The gun went bang
The leopard went down.

Eden Pullan (12)
Holy Family RC & CE College, Heywood

The Blue Sea

What is this wet thing?
It smashes against the river,
And it roars very loudly,

The sea animals,
Love to play in the blue sea,
Ow a jellyfish.

The shells are washed up,
Here upon the sandy shore,
I collect the shells.

The people love to fish,
But put the fish on their dish,
And eat it up.

I swim in the sea,
With the crabs following me,
What is this wet thing?

The sharks have big teeth,
They eat up little people,
For their tea yum, yum.

The seahorses laugh,
And sometimes they have a blast,
The seahorses jump.

The starfish they spread,
Upon the sandy shore,
They have 5 long legs.

The crabs they like to nip,
But then they hide in their shells,
And they run home.

There are some big whales,
And there are very big sizes,
They do not eat fish.

What is this wet thing?
It smashes against the river,
And it roars very loudly.

Libby Partington (12)
Holy Family RC & CE College, Heywood

Floods

The water streams downtown like a load of tears.
Just like the victims that lost their sweet homes.
It was worth a lot but they lost it all.
They search the street trying to find a place.
Just know floods will never bring back what's lost.

It has hidden everything from them.
In a wet flow leading down the long stream.
Making the noise whoosh, whoosh tormenting.
It cares about no one or their objects.
All it wants is to change their lives for bad.

It destroys their life and takes some as well.
Religion says 'it's a sign from our god'
While other people are a load of pigs.
And they don't care about what has happened.
Simply because it isn't them in pain.

But washed-out memories will not come back.
The job is done as the screams take more away.
Like lava coming out of a volcano.
Fast at the start but carries on slowly.
People watch and stare watching it take them.

Just you staring away at lost friends.
But cry away as the stream carries on.
Making itself longer by the minute.
It's dangerous and kills many people.
But cry a river just like the river.

It flows fast, deadly and very cruel.
It will carry on crying every day.
Look from its point of view, it just wants friends,
It can never get, because it destroys.
It doesn't mean to though, it is a curse.

Ashleigh Haigh (13)
Holy Family RC & CE College, Heywood

Alone

She walks down the corridor,
No one really knows,
What actually happens,
When she walks home,

Her phone invaded,
With messages from them,
Telling her she's worthless,
Nothing to them.

She sits at home
Crying every night
'I didn't do anything,
How is this right?'

The bully isn't big
They're really small
The worst thing is
They don't know each other at all.

Caitlin Allan (11)
Holy Family RC & CE College, Heywood

Law

People everywhere committing crime,
The police can be all around,
Bringing criminals in for a long time,
Criminals in jail with not one sound.

Sound of the police
Rioting on all the streets
Will someone stop this?

Law and order may be true,
With all the crimes being committed
The cops with their new blue
They will be here for a long time so criminals be ready to admit it.

Calum Kinsella (13)
Holy Family RC & CE College, Heywood

Family Poem

My family is big,
altogether is seven,
And there are five kids,
as funny as Alonso.

We all love our mum,
she is very lovely,
She looks after us,
mum makes it look so easy.

Corey is fifteen,
he is as tall as a giant,
But he is heavy,
he's growing to be like dad.

Caitlan is thirteen,
I am a very kind girl,
I have four brothers,
they are confident.

Kai is eight years old,
he looks out for us too much,
He dresses smart too,
Kai takes after me and mum.

Alonso is fun,
he is cheeky, clumsy too,
Don't take after him,
Alonso will make you laugh.

Darrius is cute,
you will love him like my mum,
He looks up to me,
however he is moody.

My dad left my mum,
he packed his stuff and left us,
Corey, mum, Caitlan,
Also he never came back.

My family poem,
I hope you enjoyed it too,
Facts about family,
especially my dad's side.

Caitlan Tiffany (13)
Holy Family RC & CE College, Heywood

Winds With Floods

Water
Water around
Rivers are like big pools
Floods are spreading very quickly.
Hurry!

Go quick
Underwater
It's now like an island.
To be safe evacuate please.
Go now.

Army
Help we need you.
Doors are at high risks, please.
The winds are tearing them apart
Careful.

Football
Football cancelled
Too dangerous go home.
It would be better for you please
Go home.

Fallen
Fallen trees, stuck
It's now too dangerous
Winter, too cold, too frosty now
Not fair.

Bethany Noon (13)
Holy Family RC & CE College, Heywood

All Alone

Not a roof over my head,
Not even a big comfy bed

No money to spare,
People wouldn't care

Freezing cold always,
carrying a heavy load

No food, no water,
carrying my 5-year-old daughter

Can't sleep at night,
my body filled with fright.

All alone, with no home.

Liam Christodoulides (12)
Holy Family RC & CE College, Heywood

The Law

The law today is bad,
the news says it's all rad.
People getting off scot-free,
when they are guilty.

Why are they let free,
when they are guilty ?

People get arrested for being on public property,
when dangerous people get let free.

Improve the law,
for humanity.

Joseph Vickers (11)
Holy Family RC & CE College, Heywood

The Kiddy Law Made By Kids

Adults have rules,
OAPs have rules,
teenagers have rules,
but nobody knows the kiddie rules!

Written in a book,
hidden in a place where no one will look.
Only to be found to this date.
It states . . .

Don't make them work.
Don't give them detentions,
let them play late at night,
that's how to do it right!

Don't punish them,
play with them,
spoil them,
help them.
Do their homework for them.

Don't give them veg
Don't push off the edge
Don't even push them in a hedge

Don't use them as bait,
let them play with their mates.
Give them choc choc.
Don't keep them under lock.

And that's that!

Caitlin Garner (11)
Holy Family RC & CE College, Heywood

Untitled

There was sloth with his toy cloth,
He waddled through the white blanket snow,
He looked up to see the sky flashing green and red and blue and pink,
It looked very majestic and had all the colours of the rainbow,
The sloth felt warm and happy inside,
The crunchy snow crunches under his feet,
and he happily walked home into the eternal burning horizon!

Ethan Izzo (13)
Holy Family RC & CE College, Heywood

Space

The stars are bright, the sun is light.
The moon is dull, Mars is full.
Aliens are green, they can be seen.

The sky is black, meteors attack.
Spaceships fly around, they make an awful sound.
When they look at the moon, they say, 'We will plant the flag soon.'

Matthew Burton (12)
Holy Family RC & CE College, Heywood

Neptune

N ever close,
E ver for,
P ulling away from the star,
T hough never discovered a lot is known,
U nrealised not a lot has been shown,
N eptune, ever the glimmer in our system,
E ternally spinning in time and in fiction.

Callum Anderson
Holy Family RC & CE College, Heywood

Too Cool For School

Walking around the playground seeing kids being silly,
watching the teacher spanking Billy,
feeling sorry for the geeky kids being laughed at,
scared of the teacher who we class as the old bat,
being stared at by the gaggle of girls giving dirty looks.

Oh please I'm no fool
I'm way to cool for school!

Comforting the girl with mascara down her face,
cheering for your siblings winning the race,
screaming at your phone because flappy bird won't fly,
leaving primary saying your last goodbye.

Oh please I'm no fool
I'm way too cool for school!

Georgia Humphery (12)
Holy Family RC & CE College, Heywood

Global Warming

You are the planet I live on,
I wake up to see you every day and I smile,
when you get hurt so do I.

You are the reason I live,
Cars drive past and I think why?
Why harm the environment if one day you won't be here?

What will we do once you have gone?

Respect our world,
Respect you responsibilities to care for the environment.

Stop harming our world!

Philippa Cordwell (12)
Holy Family RC & CE College, Heywood

What Have They Done?

Shooting birds, killing doves,
destroying all the things we love,
chopping off tails, stepping on snails,
no more are the humpback whales.

Cutting down trees, poisoning seas,
forcing us back down on our knees,
cutting bones, standing alone,
children mourning, crying for their phones.

So let this be a lesson for the next race,
for we are no more,
our confidence was our downfall.

Don't chop the trees, don't kill the roosters,
you must work together,
to create a brighter future.

Jamie Shepherd (12)
Holy Family RC & CE College, Heywood

Bullying

She is alone, in need of a friend.
All the bullying never ends.
No matter how hard she tries,
she can't help but cry.
She has no one to comfort her,
her life is just a lonely blur.
She tries to make friends,
she tries to fit in,
but she never wins.
What's the point? There is none.
Everyone get along and have *fun*!

Ashlea Winborne (11)
Holy Family RC & CE College, Heywood

The Girl Who Is Always Alone

Everything is black in her life.
Everyone hates her it's not very nice.
Her life is hated, she has been brought down.
As she walks down the path, she gets stared at by the whole town.
She is different from everyone else, she sits by herself.
She works by herself, she is completely alone.
She changes herself and tries to fit in, but she can never win the friendship around her.
She walks home alone and every day there are messages on her phone, breaking her heart and making her feel down.
Every day is the same for her, no one seems to change,
but she tells herself that 'there's nothing to do except for living life by being strange'.

Tonya Ashworth (11)
Holy Family RC & CE College, Heywood

Snow!

Snow is cold and cruel, suffocating our world in ice,
Yet as it lays its perfect coat of white; the scenery can be rather nice,
Wrapping up in layers of fur, no animals to be heard, maybe a tweet or a purr,
Roast chicken floats through an open door, beckoning me to take the turn,
Wafts of snow drizzle down on me, as I stride out into the night . . . I feel free,
Finally able to explore the wonders of the world,
I take off, up a mountain with the highest build.
The snow, covering this mountain as a blanket.
My mother closes the book, smiles and says goodnight -
Wrapping me up in a blanket I know I'll sleep safe and tight.

Leona Whittle (12)
Holy Family RC & CE College, Heywood

Falling Into Darkness

The day was grey,
but just for her.
Cuts on her wrists,
she was hurt

It wasn't fair,
mascara down her face,
no one understood.
She couldn't keep her pace.

Suicide: it calls her closer,
it calls her near.
Death whispers down her ear . . .

She's tried.
She's thrived.
But yet,
It presides;
this feeling inside.

Anger and rage devour her,
alone in her cave.
All she wants is to be free.
But she couldn't be brave.

It's hard, it's tough.
She's not enough.

Amelia Holt
Holy Family RC & CE College, Heywood

Aboard The Carrier (Villanelle Poem)

The alarm screams loud after night,
The game has started,
They're all ready, so let's fight.

The engines roar in all their might,
The pilot jumps in ready for war,
The Mustangs are ready for their flight.

For days and days it was not right,
They stayed inside the ship,
They're all ready, so let's fight.

On land or sea, day or night,
Permanently awake,
The Mustangs are ready for their flight.

While below deck it is alright,
But, above life is hard,
They're all ready, so let's fight.

On land our soldiers fought and fought,
People killed, people hurt,
They sold their lives to our country,
They were all ready, so let's fight.

Sam Milne (13)
Holy Family RC & CE College, Heywood

The Bat, The Cat And The Smelly Old Rat

Once there was a bat
He was a jolly old tool
He had one love and that was the cat

The cat lived on a mat
It was warm and glittering like a jewel
The cat invited the bat over to her cosy old mat

The bat replied yes, after a little chat
He wore his suit he looked so cool
And don't forget his hat

They both sat
He gave her a beautiful jewel
And grew a little fat

Along came the smelly old rat
His eyes lit up to the jewel
The bat hid the jewel but he stole his hat

That little brat
What a tool
He pulled a gun out and shot him to the head; he was now a dead rat
So don't steal and break the law; don't be a rat.

Thomas Rooney (13)
Holy Family RC & CE College, Heywood

The Waiter: Villanelle

Every year it must return:
Here, there, everywhere,
Unwanted, not a place to turn.

A quaint day off yet to earn,
Always present nobody could care,
Unfair but never learns.

The pain goes, never to return
But they don't know it will always be there.
Will they ever learn?

It won't disappear, the flame will always burn
In a flash, it will appear
In every corner, every turn.

Any victim it will never learn
So quick, no time to spare
Visits once never to return

Ensuring the fallen don't return
Empty bodies, bare
No movement, not a turn
Take their souls, watch them burn.

Wil Rowley (12)
Holy Family RC & CE College, Heywood

Stepping Into A Cloud

The day was hard and long,
She wondered what went wrong.

She couldn't take any more,
as she fell to the floor!

All that was saw was a blade
She began to get hot enough for the fire brigade.

Her cuts open bare,
it wasn't fair.

Sadness came back,
like a long-lost friend.
She wished it would stay,
yet she wished it would end.

Surrounded by darkness,
drowning in sorrow.
She went to sleep,
but wouldn't wake tomorrow.

Just one more cut on her wrist or thigh.
Just one step closer to goodbye.

Olivia Moseley (12)
Holy Family RC & CE College, Heywood

Little Emo Me

Now and forever,
Till death do us part?
That will come sooner,
That will come now,
I want to die
And don't give two bulls
Whether you care or not.
But listen to me . . .
I know some care
But my life is hell.
So if you do give a bull
Just know you weren't the cause.
My depression.
My hell.
Was caused by them . . .
The populars,
Them pretties,
The jocks,
Them idiots,
The perfect people.
The witches with a capital B.
The worst part is . . .
My family helped.
Not caring.
Not giving a bull.
But you don't care and I certainly don't.
So don't mourn, don't cry
Unless you truly cared about
Little Emo Me.

Jessica Adshead (14)
Kingsthorpe College, Northampton

Rest My Soft Head

Every day I walk to my lonely bed,
I lie down and rest my soft head,
For when I look out my window, I can see the stars twinkling and beginning to dance.

For every day I walk to my bed,
I realise I'm not dead,
For when I walk to my lonely bed, I lie down and rest my soft head.

The wind is bitter and the window is unsealed,
I hear a whisper but nothing is revealed,
So I go back to sleep but take another peep; still nothing is there, and nothing quite dead.

But every day I walk to my lonely bed,
I look out my lonely window and rest my soft head and
Realise I am still not quite dead.

Pirez Liburd-Hamilton (12)
Kingsthorpe College, Northampton

Love Lost

Life comes and goes as it pleases,
you have left my heart in pieces,
time is meant to be a healer with all this pain.
Will my life ever feel the same?
I have a space in my heart that when you left you tore apart.
One day we will meet again until that day the pain will remain.

Aaliyah Rolfe-Lovatt (11)
Kingsthorpe College, Northampton

My Upside Down World A-Z

I can see an antelope following a yellow brick road
I can see a bear playing with a toad
I can see a cat eyeing a mouse on a roof
I can see a dog polishing a horse's hoof
I can see an elephant climbing into a tree
I can see a frog trying not to sneeze
I can see a gorilla painting a picture so tall
I can see a hyena catching a bus to school
I can see an iguana wearing top brand clothes
I can see a jaguar miraculously blowing his nose
I can see a kangaroo happily having a laugh
I can see a lion having a long hot bath
I can see a monkey doing the awesome crab walk
I can see a newt learning how to talk
I can see an octopus climbing the Eiffel Tower
I can see a parrot having a shower
I can see a quail watching HDTV
I can see a reindeer jumping into the sea
I can see a slug having a dance
I can see a turkey travelling to France
I can see an umbrella bird singing in the choir
I can see a vulture trying to bite a wire
I can see a whale prancing with a mouse
I can see an X-ray fish jumping into a house
I can see a yak getting into the door
I can see a zebra mopping up the floor
I can see my bedroom wall . . . *wow* . . . I must be dreaming!

Dylan Storey (14)
Kingsthorpe College, Northampton

The Zombies Are Back Again

The zombies are insane,
They enjoy human brains,
The blood and gore swipes the floor,
The zombies are back again!

Oh no they're here!
Why are they so sinister!
I pack my bags, hide stuff under my rag,
The zombies are back again!

Grab a gun, call my friend,
but no one answers,
In the dark, I hear dogs bark,
The zombies are back again!

Shot a head or two,
It wasn't something new,
I ran as fast as I can,
Packed my stuff inside a van,
The zombies are back again!

They've swarmed me!
I hear the blood drops,
I wish it would stop,
Nothing to do, my gun's out of ammo,
The zombies are back again!

Goran Milivojevic (11)
Kingsthorpe College, Northampton

Life

Life is full of ups and downs,
Full of smiles and also frowns,
Some are rich and some are poor,
Some are kicked right out the door.

People born day after day,
Happily on their mothers they lay,
Then there's death they're no longer here,
Last words are: I love you dear.

Lots of houses big and small,
Wish there was one for us all,
On the streets some people lay,
People laughing at them day after day.

Some lives are good some are bad,
Looking at others wishing they had,
Some people fortunate, unfortunate too,
I'm happy with my life and what I do.

Jamie Allen (11)
Kingsthorpe College, Northampton

What's Education?

Sometimes I wonder, did education lose its voice,
or did we give it no choice?
I wonder and start to think, will pen and paper help you,
later in life and in its quests?
I think the hardest part is teachers wanting to see our success.
They want us to hold the key to our future.
Well don't forget that teachers were once students too,
and don't forget that every problem or question you create,
we have to solve or answer to see our success,
and help us in the future.
Many issues face students and teachers, so think to yourself,
are we all going to change for the future?

Laura Aggett
Kingsthorpe College, Northampton

The Boxing Ring

The punch flew
And then I knew
It was time to stand tall
Or shrink and fall

The punch flew
And then I knew
It was time to duck and weave
And make my opponent want to leave

The punch flew
And then I knew
It was time to block
And give him a real shock

The punch flew
And then I knew
My opponent was weak
And no longer at his peak

My punch flew
And then I knew
It was time to claim my victory
My opponent was history.

Owen Campbell (12)
Kingsthorpe College, Northampton

Loved Ones

You don't know how much you love them until they're gone
Why do you have to leave for so long?
I really don't understand
But we all hold hand in hand
To support our grieving hearts.

Abigail Francis (13)
Kingsthorpe College, Northampton

I Love The Rainforest

I love the rainforest
I love the rainforest
I love the rainforest

Toucans fly,
And lazy leopards lie,
I love the rainforest

The muddy floor is brown
And the waterfall gushes down
I love the rainforest

The river shines bright
And the midges bite
I love the rainforest

Spiders crawl and creep
And frogs jump and leap
I love the rainforest

Green plants grow
And the winds may blow
I love the rainforest.

Streams flow fast
Birds fly past
I love the rainforest.

Temperatures are mostly hot
But just fear not
Because I love the rainforest

Species are rare
But I don't care
Because I love the rainforest

I love the rainforest
I love the rainforest
I love the rainforest.

Alicia Jeyes (12)
Kingsthorpe College, Northampton

Snow

It's time for some snow
Put away that lilo
It's all covered white,
What a big delight.
Time to build a snowman.
No more suntan.
Let's have a snowball fight,
Up until midnight.
Let's make some stew
Instead of a barbeque.
Wipe away that tear,
It will be back again next year.

Charlie Philora (13)
Kingsthorpe College, Northampton

Broke

Torn down home
No one to go to
You wish you would see
What you have to go through
Every day is a war
Knowing you can't take any more
Family broke and so are you
If only they would see what you have to go through
Love is pain
Pain to you
Please see what I go through.

Bethan Gookey
Kingsthorpe College, Northampton

Chocolate

I like chocolate.
Chocolate goes bang, crunch, pop.
Sugary sweetness

Melting in my mouth,
My taste buds dance like crazy -
Gooey caramel

Sticky caramel,
Bitter Bournville chocolate,
Bounties drive me nuts

Snickers are so nice,
Snickers are really nutty,
Give me one more slice.

Fauzia Sattar (13)
Kingsthorpe College, Northampton

Sadness

As we look around the battlefields
We watch the birds,
the birds soar
And we wish there was no war.

The homeless lay on the cold concrete floor,
And this all happened just because they're poor
As their tears fill their eyes
Our ears are surrounded by their cries.

People die and rivers flow,
But they all have to go,
The sun is shining,
And the clock is chiming.

Sam Davies (12)
Kingsthorpe College, Northampton

Voices

They're back
Do you hear them?
Of course not.
But when I'm alone
I find myself
On the brink of sanity
I can't say anything about them
They'd hurt me
They told me
And all I want
Is for them
To stop
Because even when I cover my ears
I still hear them
because
They're back.

Bubble Atkins (12)
Kingsthorpe College, Northampton

Nans

No words can describe how great a nan is,
She has wrinkles on her face,
And rollers in her hair,
Her hair is as white as snow.
She has many personalities,
She is kind,
She is funny,
She is the one that looks after you.

She is the one person you can trust,
She is cute,
She is caring,
She is short . . .

She is my nan.

Caitlin Malone (13)
Kingsthorpe College, Northampton

Music!

Music moves all through my body,
Now I can say it is living all around me,
This is my heaven,
It puts me in a good mood.

It always makes me forget about my pain,
It brings out the sunshine when I see rain.
I put my headphones on and play all my tunes
I can listen to it all day long

Music takes me to a different place,
Higher and higher far from space,
There is nothing to compare, it's my whole world,
It is even better than a pot of gold.

Music teaches me so many lessons,
Like standing up for yourself with good reasons,
I know people feel the same way,
Because they know it is with us every day.

Isabelle Seal (11)
Kingsthorpe College, Northampton

The Fight

With this skill you have to have a heart
Because you need to be perfect at the art.
When the bell rings,
Ding, ding,
You stop and think what this will bring.
The crowd watches, tense . . .
Who will be the one walking past that fence?
A punch to the left and the right,
You know he's up for a big fight.

Lewis Patching (12)
Kingsthorpe College, Northampton

School

When school starts at eight-forty,
In that lesson no one's particularly naughty.
Maths, you find quite boring,
A few hours ago you were snoring.

At break, you feel like sleeping,
But actually you're in the canteen eating.
In the next lesson you get woken up,
By being shouted at by a teacher, called Mrs Mutt.

At lunch, everyone else is eating,
But you forgot your lunch, so you are starving.
In the last period everyone is tired, and feels like going home,
Just to get into bed.

You wake up the next morning
To do it again.

Matty Slinn (12)
Kingsthorpe College, Northampton

Sonnet On Food

Cookies and pizza, oh what a delight,
This is a poem of how I love food
Food weakens me, just like kryptonite,
It also puts me in a happy mood.
Some food I like include pasta and rice,
Starchy food has a place inside my heart,
Sugar and spice just everything nice.
All the store, it finds a way into my cart
Hunger always keeping me at bay,
With three meals a day and snacks between.
My mum said with my food 'don't play'
Basically food is special to me,
I eat all of the time as you can see.

Abbie Wood
Kingsthorpe College, Northampton

War

Day by day, night by night, the sound of the blazing
guns echoes off the drums of my ears
with each breath I take there's
pain and suffering, the sound of my men and my friends
replay in my head over and over like a broken
record, I close my eyes, I can't fall asleep.
The images of dying enemies and foes haunts me freezing my spine
my mind, my soul, the things I have seen have been images from
Hell put in by the Devil himself, wishing them to be ripped
out of my head, I can take no more.
With each bullet I put into that mag
fires out of the barrel killing an unfortunate soldier in front, we may be
very different but we are all soldiers without an army.
Forgotten, alone, abandoned.
We kill, we fight, we don't learn. Why do we fight? Why do we kill?
Why don't we learn?
So we evolve as a person so we have our
victory, our humanity,
our freedom.

James Thompson
Kingsthorpe College, Northampton

Nature, Nature

Nature, nature
Look around you
Hear the birds tweet
Listen to the heartbeat
Never have I been in awe!

The butterflies' wings
The bluebird sings
Our eyes will widen
You'll see!
So never fear
For nature is near
And find its delight in the year!

Kelis Darko
Kingsthorpe College, Northampton

Rivers

The river is a runner,
That runs on the river bed,
Where sea birds fly and sea creatures roar,
The river on going like a wild boar.

The river's like a shiny mirror,
It reflects images seen throughout life,
The river rolls stones like a dice,
When winter comes, it turns into ice.

The river is like a God,
It watches over everything that passes,
The waters are whisked off the boat's oar,
Freedom to float runs with the streamline.

Luke Smith-Whelan (14)
Kingsthorpe College, Northampton

My Thoughts

My thoughts are a heaven and a hell.

My thoughts are my hopes and dreams.
My thoughts are the things I hoped would never happen.

My thoughts are where I want to end up.
My thoughts are where I want to avoid.

My thoughts are a collection of jokes.
Not all of them good.

My thoughts remind me of my greatest moments.
My thoughts remind me of the times I wished I was not alive.

My thoughts and memories could never save my legs
But without them I wouldn't be here today.

Adam Stopher (12)
Kingsthorpe College, Northampton

Wolves

The wolves are always coming,
They are coming right away,
If we don't move quickly I think we'll have to play,
The wolves are going to get me,
They can smell my fear,
They are camouflaged in the snow and ice,
Their motive is unclear,
What is the price I'll have to pay,
If I dice with death,
Then I'll get cut,
Time to get out of here,
The wolves are coming,
The wolves have got me,
I'm done for!

Zak Deacon (13)
Kingsthorpe College, Northampton

Silence

Their words will drive me mad
by playing a loop in my head.
The fears that hide beneath
are the same secrets that I keep.
I want to be left alone
but silence is something no one knows.
I can always hear the noises that I want to lose.
And it toys with my head.
Playing on a tape with words unsaid.
The sounds haunt me
Till my death.

Erin Garlick
Kingsthorpe College, Northampton

Why I Live?

I live for my brother, my father, my mother.
I live for my nanny, my pappy, my friends.
I live for my uncles, my aunties and cousins.
I live to make memories, to share to the end.
I live for the universe.
I live for the stars.
I live because I want to, not because I can.
I live to love and love to live.
I live for a reason words cannot explain.
I live another day to try and succeed and even to fail.
I live another day to understand why.
Why the birds sing, why the dogs bark?
Why our parents are our parents?
Why we fall in love and why we fall out of it?
Why do some hate Marmite, why do some love it?
Why do we have Easter and Christmas?
Why do we sleep in a bed?
Why does one of us end up dead?
And why do we believe in life after death?
My mum is my hero.
My dad is my life.
My brother is my beacon of light.
My best friend is like a sister.
My sister is my friend.
My laughter is my comforter.
My happiness is my life.
My life is my world.
That's why I live it . . .

Bethany Gates (12)
Kingsthorpe College, Northampton

Creep

You hurt your daughters
You hurt your wife
I hope you stay
In jail for life

You wrecked 3 families
Including mine
I'm trying to convince people
That I'm fine

But I'm not
It's not easy to see
You violated children
Especially me

You're a creep
That's what you are
Your actions
Did not get you far

15 months in prison
And you're still lying
If it was up to me
You'd be slowly dying

Every day I awake screaming
As I see you in my sleep
All you're after is attention
That is what you seek

You try to change your story
Over and over again
But everyone knows the truth
So then

You're a creep
You're a creep.

Abigayle Caborn (13)
Kingsthorpe College, Northampton

The One I Miss

The one I miss is my nan,
No she is not dead but very ill.
I cannot explain how much I miss
But I can claim my love.

She is great I love her so,
She is the best, I love her so, because she is my nan.
I have much sympathy for my mum,
As she is in pain the most.

As again, I love her as she loved me.
She came with hugs and her loving kiss.
I love my nan,
She is the best.
The best there is.

George Watson (12)
Kingsthorpe College, Northampton

Our Generation

Our generation is more interested in
Looks than what's on the inside.

Our generation is more interested in
'What Does the Fox Say' than they are in Syria.

Our generation is more interested in
The latest games than they are in terrorism.

Our generation is more interested in
Themselves than they are in the
Soldiers that fight for freedom.

Our generation needs fixing.
Our generation has to be changed.

Shauna Calpin
Kingsthorpe College, Northampton

Cold Night

Cold night, out of sight stay the children of the night,
Hungry, sad, feeling bad without anything to eat . . .
Parents gone, they sit alone,
On the terrifying cold night, begging, crying . . .
'Please give me some money'.
People passing, just one coin,
They will not give . . .
Their selfish ways of life
'Please give me some money' they just keep passing,
Guilty
'Those dirty children want drugs, don't they?' they say,
But one little coin, they will not give . . .

Sit in sight, but still at night the children do,
'Please, I beg you, I need some money', people pass,
Some people smile,
'You shouldn't have wasted it' they laugh . . .

All alone the children roam,
Wanting to go home, but a home,
They do not have . . .
They die, they cry, but no one cares.

Marcel Nowakowski (13)
Kingsthorpe College, Northampton

Love

I hate the way you smile at me
I hate the way you cook tea.
I hate the way you make me laugh
And the way you wear that checkered scarf.
I hate the way you always think you're right
'cause we always end up in a fight.
I hate the way that you work in a zoo
I hate the fact that I love you.

Millie Sharpe
Kingsthorpe College, Northampton

The Time Of Fasting

In the holy month Ramadan,
the moon rises,
and we start a fantastic day

Every single Muslim,
fasts and prays

We love our religion so much,
it will stay in our hearts

We invite each othcr,
break our fasts,
and have a party with delicious,
mouth-watering food

We had the best fun,
and stayed in a happy mood,
for 30 days

Who have a big celebration,
with fancy clothes,
which is called Eid

Hopefully our prayers,
and our wishes will all
Succeed!

Habibah Hannan (12)
Kingsthorpe College, Northampton

Anaconda

Slowly, slithering, elegantly,
The snake smells its prey.
Moving undetected, it strikes,
Devouring its prey with its powerful jaws.
You can see its prey digested
In its powerful, digestive juices . . .

Cameron Cheer (11)
Kingsthorpe College, Northampton

The Plague

Run, flee you can't stay here,
Eternal sleep and death is near,
Evil, cruel and hatred-filled,
Cities full of people killed.

Its stare spreads disease with one look,
It's awful all the lives it took,
No knife, no dagger only death.
Handing people their final breath.

Run, flee you can't stay here,
Eternal sleep and death is near.
Evil, cruel and hatred-filled
Cities full of people killed.

Stealing life, stealing souls,
Broken hearts as black as coal,
Thump! Another body drops to the floor,
Skin all lumpy and sore.

Run, flee you can't stay here,
Eternal sleep and death is near,
Evil, cruel and hatred-filled,
Cities full of people killed.

It's hand is a gun, shooting out life
Causing havoc, causing strife
The plague is coming
Run!

Belle Skelton (12)
Kingsthorpe College, Northampton

Winter Dance

The blue sky went and said goodbye,
as the white winter sky popped into my eye.
The winter was finally here,
I am so happy and full of cheer.
As I stepped onto the ice rink,
the dancers began to sync.
They dance and glide with all their might
Then I slide on with my crazy stage fright.
We lightly glide along the ice,
wearing fancy clothes we all look nice.
Turning around and jumping high,
makes us feel like we can fly.
We can't see the audience which feels strange,
because the lights are bright and they always change.
The music is blaring it's very loud,
we're smiling, we're happy, we're very proud.
We slide, we glide, we do the big jump,
The dance was a success not even a bump.
The dance is finished the crowd is screaming,
we're so happy our faces are gleaming.
It's time to go home we had fun,
out in the snow we love to run.
We jump and lay in the snow,
It's like another winter dance for us to show.

Sherry Daniels (13)
Kingsthorpe College, Northampton

Star Of Strength

The night has come, but not just yet,
And sinking silently,
All silently, the little moon,
Drops down behind the sky,
There is no light in earth or Heaven,
but just the cold light of stars,
and the first watch of night is given,
to the red planet Mars,
O star of strength, I see you stand,
and you smile upon my pain,
you gave me light and bravery in my hand,
And I am now strong again,
O star of strength, I thank you . . .

Georgie Williams
Kingsthorpe College, Northampton

A Dream Upon Clouds

I drift away in the clouds, a fantasy of the eternal splendour of the sky
Sense your soul, sense your heartbeat as the clouds cry in pain
I'll reach out to the blazing stars upon stars as a life passes by
Howling clouds can only precipitate nothing more but words hurt as much as actions
Excruciating torture day by day not a second may pass to attain your passions
Forgotten, erased, elapsed in your closed eye wonderland
I dream of happiness, a life without struggle, a place named Neverland,
I'm stuck in Heaven, imprisoned, deprived, dejected, good or bad only you can decide,
I feel I will wake one day,
but the real world, filled with agony and sorrow, is the true nightmare,
once upon a time, you can run away from fears, once upon a time you will understand,
No matter what they say,
keep your dreams but don't dream your life away.

Saheem Islam (13)
Kingsthorpe College, Northampton

The Rain

Drip, drop
Went the rain on the rooftops.
Crashing down from the skies above,
Drowning out the sun we love.

Puddles gather by the side of the road,
Soaking shoppers carrying their load.
When the cars drive by and create a splash,
Pedestrians run, speed and dash.

We certainly don't want it to thunder,
Will this rain ever stop I wonder?
Flooding is destroying our homes,
Without the sun it is unknown,
What will happen to our lives?
Will we be able to survive?

As much as we appreciate you, rain,
Sometimes you are just a pain!
Our lives are like a living hell,
When you will stop no one can tell.

Phoebe Horne (13)
Kingsthorpe College, Northampton

Love

Love can be sweet
Love can be sour
Love is like a wild fire
Love is a storm
Love calls out to you
Love lives inside of you
Love is the spark of a relationship
Love starts the fire
Love makes the bond
Love seals the bond
What can your love do?

Brandon McVicker (13)
Kingsthorpe College, Northampton

Sports

Sport inspires us,
to compete
Winning over losing,
is much more sweet.
Baseball, football and basketball,
are fun.
Let's grab some friends,
and play in the sun.
In football, you pass the ball,
using your feet.
Drinking plenty of water,
and watching out for the heat.
In basketball the best sound,
is a swish,
Making ten in a row,
is a wonderful wish.
In baseball you will be,
running around.
When you hit the ball it is,
a beautiful sound.
Whatever sport you decide to play,
enjoy them with your friends every day.

Caitlyn Robinson (11)
Kingsthorpe College, Northampton

Football

My socks are grass stained
The sun is shining across the field
My toes are cold
I can hear people calling for the ball
The ball rolls to my feet
I run closer to the goal
I strike the ball
And it hits the pole!

Bradley Gibson (13)
Kingsthorpe College, Northampton

Taken

Taken away from my brother
I cried
Taken away from my mother
I died
Now, I am standing in the dark,
Playing in the park.
I see this man,
Beside a white van.
I start to run,
But he has a gun.
I was in pain as it started to rain.
He took a step closer
Then another
Then I said goodbye to my
Mother.

Mia Sales (13)
Kingsthorpe College, Northampton

The Fall

Summer has gone and autumn is here,
the growing season has finished, the harvest is near,
shadows grown long, sun low in the sky,
there is a chill in the air the plant life has died,
wrap up warm for a walk in the woods,
gloves, scarves and coats with hoods,
the forest is silent migrant birds flown away,
beautiful colours for a short while will stay,
crisp morning mists evenings drawing dark,
children collecting conkers playing in the park,
leaves have started falling a special time of the year,
the winter is approaching with festivities and cheer.

Tayla Gillingham (14)
Kingsthorpe College, Northampton

My Shoe's Day

Playing football is fun to do.
But sometimes I lose my shoe.
I kick the ball with all my might.
But my shoe is not very tight.
So I can only watch it take flight.

Higher and higher into the air. '*That's my shoe!*'
I shout in despair.
The ball I kicked is out of play.
It's my shoe that scored *hooray!*
My shoe's the highlight of the game.
And now I'm the one to blame.
For the goalkeeper on the ground
Cried when my shoe knocked him down.

Luke Duffy (12)
Kingsthorpe College, Northampton

Summertime

The splash of cold water that hits in the face,
refreshing and cool,
with an ice cream in my hand,
I walk by the pool.

Time to go to the beach,
time to go and chill,
time to have a bottle of water,
time to have a sunbathe.

The warm, crystal clear water beckoned me in,
time to take a dip in the ocean,
as I walk towards the water,
I saw stretches of golden sands going along the warm Cornish beach

'Time to go! It's been a long day!' my parents say.
I sigh and look one last time behind me.
Bye paradise, bye Cornwall,
See you next year.

Alicia Woolard (11)
Kingsthorpe College, Northampton

Clouds

You sit on the clouds,
As I watch them float by,
Your smile the reflection,
In the sun,
In the sky.

Up in the clouds,
No harm can be done.
Life is much easier,
Also more fun.

It was painful,
But all is at rest,
Knowing you're there,
The feeling is best.

Clouds are like candyfloss,
fluffy,
light,
I look at them hoping they are never out of sight,
for my vision of you,
dancing above,
makes me sing a sweet song,
for you, sister my love.

When it gets tough,
I look to the clouds
Because I know that you are there,

For forever and a year,
Sister my dear.

Rachel Liburd
Kingsthorpe College, Northampton

Night

Breathe, just breathe I tell myself,
I wish I was asleep,
Breathe, just breathe I tell myself
I hope this is a dream.

Light is gone, night is here,
People fear this time,
The shadows dance and raise the dead
I can't get the picture out of my head,

Breathe, just breathe I tell myself,
I wish I was asleep,
Breathe, just breathe I tell myself,
I hope this is a dream,

Please, please don't be real,
When will day come?
The moon can't help but just watch
And listen to the yells,

Breathe, just breathe I tell myself,
I wish I was asleep,
Breathe, just breathe I tell myself
I hope this is a dream.

Bang, bang I hear the door
Oh no they are coming for me
I hear a slither then a snap
A shadow is staring at me.

Brooke Gillingham (12)
Kingsthorpe College, Northampton

Music Poem

Music can make you sad,
Music can make happy,
Music can be about things that are bad,
Some music can even make you go yappy.

Music makes you want to dance,
Music makes you want to sing,
Even if people glance,
You don't care you just want to sing,
a-ring-a-ding-ding.

Music can be about romance,
Music can be about hate,
Music can be about making you see sense,
Music can be about spite.

When you listen to music, what to you hear?
When you listen to music, do you feel fear?
When you listen to music do you start crying,
or do you hear people sighing?
I've made up my mind,
what do you find?

Kristie Foster
Kingsthorpe College, Northampton

The Tragic News

On my way from school
I was feeling really cool
I've had a happy day
Then my dad drove me home all they way
He looked really sad
Was there something bad?
My brother came in the car
Then Dad drove us far
He told me some tragic news
That I wished I had refused
I heard about my grandad's day
When his life faded away
Tears were shared
About my grandad's death
Dad said, 'Don't cry.
Your grandad's fate is within the sky.'
He was always loved
But he's in the heavens above . . .

Niyaz Rahman
Kingsthorpe College, Northampton

Family!

I have my mum's height, my father's anger,
my brother's passion, the other's hunger,

And when the youngest started to speak,
I realised we shared a stubborn streak.

So I may be round and he may be slim,
Dad may be clever and Mum may be dim,

Although we constantly fight,
in difficult times we unite.

This is the meaning of family:
I love them and they love me!

Fatima Miah (14)
Kingsthorpe College, Northampton

My Niece

My niece is small and calm,
When I hold her in my arms.
She wakes up in the night,
Whilst developing her sight,
She is a beauty to behold,
When I protect her from the cold.

But then there's the poo!
How well did I do?
I hope I did well,
Cos oh my gosh that's one nasty smell!
Honestly what does she eat?
That nearly knocked me off my feet!

Now there's the constant disturbing!
I know she's still learning,
But I have work to do,
I say, 'I cannot play with you'
So I give her a cuddle,
Even after the struggle,

Despite all the issues,
I put away the tissues,
And forgive her blessed heart,
Because there's a part of me,
That knows what a loving uncle I can be.

Aaron Saull (13)
Kingsthorpe College, Northampton

Darkness Over

Despair, fear and grief.
They all visit tonight.
My heart is frozen, my feelings gone numb.
If only I could see the light.

Anger, rage and loss
They are old friends of mine.
My eyes are blinded, my thoughts locked.
The edge to madness becomes a thin line.

Pain, crazy and sorrow
Just leave me alone.
My memories are clear.
My future clouded.
Destination yet unknown.

Doubt, captivity and desperation
Have just arrived.
My soul is lost, my love has croaked.
Don't know if it can be reprieved.
Loneliness, hate and revenge
Have no secrets for me
My hope crumbled, my spirit breaking
Darkness sees its opportunity.

Sadness, agony and misery
Come to stay
My courage grows dim, my strength is melting
The light inside me fades away.

Sydney Oware (14)
Kingsthorpe College, Northampton

Wwii

The clock struck twelve
The moon was shining bright.
There was silence
Hitler's army flew across the
British sky,
The battle was about to
Commence.

People try to hide in a
Frightful mode
Bangs hit the ground
Child screams for his
Mother.
In the pitch-black

The loud siren rang to warn
They are here!
Spotlights hit the Nazi planes
Crash!

A young man is hit
Someone cried
His wife ran over
In tears
He's dead
She cried sadly
Heartbroken
People crying, people dying
As they're in the war.

Kimberley Osborne (11)
Kingsthorpe College, Northampton

Holiday Travel

The cases are packed and by the door
We're all excited and wondering if we should take more
In the morning to the airport we will go
Tonight is going to go slow
4 o'clock the alarm goes off
Good job Dad has got the cases out of the loft
In the car we are on the way to the airport
I read a book that I have bought
I look for signs to tell me we are nearly there
And look to see if there are any planes in the air
When we are there we go through check-in
And I have to throw my drink in the bin
We board the plane right on time
It is quarter to nine
I fasten my seat belt nice and tight
And get ready for the flight
It is not long before we are in the air
And out of the window I do stare
Below me I can see land whizzing by
I can't believe I am in the sky
Soon the pilot tells us we about to land
Excitedly I hold my Mummy's hand
The plane lands nice and soft
And now it is time to get off
The doors open and I can feel the heat
We look out for the man we are to meet
At the hotel we soon arrive
And into the pool I do dive . . .

Katie Bradshaw
Kingsthorpe College, Northampton

The White Van

I walked in the park,
It started to turn dark,
The rain was coming,
Suddenly I heard an engine humming,
A middle-aged man was driving a van,
He had a plan,
I heard primary school kids screaming,
His headlights were gleaming,
He got out of his tatty car,
He wasn't going to walk very far,
His silver key was still in,
I kicked his muddy shin,
I drove off to the police station,
I banged on the doors no answer; were they on a vacation?
I saw darkness and a man,
Oh no, I was tired and I was in the back of the van,
The sound of the engine rumbled,
My heart had just crumbled.

Al-Hadi Shah (13)
Kingsthorpe College, Northampton

War!

When you hear the deafening cry
And the soldiers pass by,
You get up and grab your gun
And you know it will not be fun,
You walk out of the door
You don't want to be here anymore,
You're dying in the trench
Wishing you were sat on a park bench

Cameron Bovingdon
Kingsthorpe College, Northampton

The Girl And The Random Boy

The room is dark,
The window brings in some light,
For us to see,
You and me,
Together forever,
Our friendship will die
Some point in time.

Here's some chocolate for you and me
Under the new Christmas tree.
As I give it to you,
Nothing to lose,
Because me and you,
Have a friendship that will never close.

The door is wide,
Open enough for a dive
In the swimming pool
Because it is cool
To be seen
Together, forever.

Byron Johnson (11)
Kingsthorpe College, Northampton

My Best Friend

There is something that keeps me and you together
and it is not tape or glue
it is our friendship that stops us being apart
I know we are apart at distance but never at heart.
I always remember the day our friendship started
and throughout the years we have never been parted.
You have never been selfish or deserted me,
even when you are as busy as a bee,
you always make time for me
and when it has been longer than it may seem,
we have always been a great team.
And there are no words to describe how much you mean to me,
no matter how hard times may have been,
or as crazy they have seemed
and all the things we have dreamed.
You are my best friend to this day and for evermore,
we shall grow stronger and more adventures will be in store,
in good or bad times you are there for me,
our friendship has never torn.
Thank you for being such a good friend of mine.
This is just a little token to thank you for all those wonderful times,
we have spent together and the adventures to come.

Kira King (13)
Kingsthorpe College, Northampton

Slave

I work all day and night
Surely this can't be right!
Gotta get back to work
Or I will get really hurt.

Being a slave for more than nine years now, can't even remember, how . . .
I think I was walking and
I saw these people talking,
I realised they were up to no good,
So I started to run as fast as I could.

But I was too late,
This time I met my fate,
Think I was beaten up
They took my bread and cup

Just because I'm black
I always get the smack.
We work all day and night,
Surely this can't be right!

Efraim Pap (11)
Kingsthorpe College, Northampton

Car

I have a passion,
Everyone says it is an obsession.
It is for Jaguar E-Types.
It is my favourite car.
I first saw it in Daventry
Which is not that far
Travelling by hours.
But the only thing I didn't like that day
Which was outside,
Was the flowers.

Ben Summers (11)
Kingsthorpe College, Northampton

I Run, I Die

I run,
It's snowing,
I cry,
Not knowing.

I'm froze,
Cold-haired,
It's close,
I'm scared.

I trip,
I bleed,
'My hip,'
I plead.

It's a man,
I cry,
There's a van
I die.

Tom Eustace (12)
Kingsthorpe College, Northampton

Friends

Friendship can be difficult in different sorts of ways
But your friend will always be there
Through all the dark and gloomy days
I love it when I see your cheeky smile
And I think about you all the while
Our friendship will last forever
And I hope we will always be together.

Hope Carter-Hands (12)
Kingsthorpe College, Northampton

Steven Gerrard

Steven Gerrard what a name
He lives within the hall of fame
A midfield man, a legend true
An Anfield player through and through.

He caresses the ball, high and low
Every week, it's quite a show
To see his skill and weight of pass
Stevie G's a different class.

An Anfield player from an early stage
Came through the ranks and learnt his trade
It didn't take him long to be
the first team player we love to see.

And here he has stayed for 15 years
A god for all the 'Kop' to cheer
A liverbird upon his chest
And three lions is his crest

From players past, all legends true,
King Kenny, Souness and Hansen too
Stevie, Anfield is your home.
And you will never walk alone.

Ross Holt (14)
Kingsthorpe College, Northampton

Snow

Snow falls softly onto the ground
Not a blade of grass to be found
Snowmen quickly start to invade
The blue skies are soon to fade

Days are spent ice skating
While the timid squirrel is hibernating
Gardens are transformed into a winter wonderland
But with everything white, it's quite bland

Sleds sell out quickly in the shops
Fingers turn into ice pops
Snow crunching under numb toes
In the distance, the Northern Lights glow

Curling up in a warm bed
'Goodbye,' winter said
'The end of this cold is near'
'Goodbye winter, until next year'.

Maisie Sproson (12)
Kingsthorpe College, Northampton

Death

Beside the dotted stars, sat Moon,
Its reflection was a silver spoon,
Upon the water, Moon stared,
At the Earth and the people it bared.

The wind whistled and it is said,
That the person who heard it was bound to be dead.
Upon the water, Moon stared,
At the Earth and the people it bared.

He heard it and looked to the skies,
Moon reflected into the pools of his eyes.
Upon the water, Moon stared,
At the Earth and the people it bared.

Salty liquid, his eyes filled,
This happened to the last victim it killed.
Upon the water, Moon stared,
At the Earth and the people it bared.

Pop! The gun fired, he fell to the floor,
Blood poured out, his heart beat no more.
Upon this water, Moon stared,
At the Earth and the person it no longer bared.

Chelsea Shatford (11)
Kingsthorpe College, Northampton

Jazz

She sleeps
She snores
She walks on all paws

She plays fetch
She plays ball
But that's not all.

She barks,
She whines
And will always be mine.

She wees,
She poos
And sometimes eats my shoes.

But I love her
And she loves me
We are one happy family.

Emily Juzyk
Kingsthorpe College, Northampton

Shopping Refund

All year
Disheartened and sad
Up all over Britain
Moving cottages
To change our doctor.

Want a refund?
The climate
Different I hated it
My shopping
To Africa opened new doors.

Isabelle Slater (13)
Kirkham Grammar Senior School, Preston

Highway Of Technology

This is the year the cat left the girl to fall on her back
Walk the ancient streets of dentists' dog
Did you know sea-floor creatures fall into my arms?
Everybody's talking about the cheeseburger of death.
Digital devices with someone behind us.
Walking through history
Supreme creepy
Ultrafast 4G or visit Everest with cats.
World war dentist
Money down the drain and staying down with unique experiments.

Maddy Cooper (13)
Kirkham Grammar Senior School, Preston

Ice Queen

Ice queen
Always mean
Forever frozen
Cold distant
Beauty perfected
Crystal clear
Inhuman statue
Without heart
Transparent soul
Lacking love
Constantly alone
Ice queen.

Kate Parkinson (11)
Kirkham Grammar Senior School, Preston

The Playground

You say, 'You name-calling nobodies,'
They say, 'Get out of my face,'
You say, 'Forget it, go please,'
They say, 'We can't share one place.'

You say, 'That slap was too hard,'
They say, 'Good I can kick you too,'
You say, 'But I'm already scared,'
They say, 'Exactly! We enjoy the view'.

You say, 'Now stop that's enough,'
They say, 'But we haven't started,'
You say, 'I'm just not that tough,'
They say, 'We know - you're faint-hearted.'

You say, 'That's it! I'm going away,'
They say, 'Yes, we've pushed you and won,'
You say, 'I'm too distraught now to stay,'
They say, 'But it was only a game, just fun.'

Emily Parkinson-Swift (16)
Kirkham Grammar Senior School, Preston

Fairy Tale

Britain's first Disney princess
Makes bathing difficulty a thing of the past.
Claim your free pack of unrequited love,
Panda's arrival hurts princes,
So go out and get a dog.
I can't tell if he's interested in me.
Boulder crashes China.
Relieve the pain and save money.
Hurry inside a camouflaged tree
Fashion young British slaves happily ever after.

Charlotte O'Neill (13)
Kirkham Grammar Senior School, Preston

Two Directions

She was out for blood
He wanted a friend
She wanted a start
He wanted to end
She wanted to kill
He wanted comfort
She didn't want to help
He didn't want to hurt
She could have been a movie star
He could have been a binman
She would have been an idol
He would have been her biggest fan
She ruined her life
He saved his own
She was sitting in jail
He finally had a home.

Molly Pickup (11)
Kirkham Grammar Senior School, Preston

Thesaurus

I'm lost in a sea of words,
The land of reality far away
Behind me, lost as I
Swim amongst ink and paper boats.
Drifting overhead are thoughtful
Clouds, twisting and twirling,
In brainstorms.

Charlotte Gee (16)
Kirkham Grammar Senior School, Preston

Global Murder

The earth is warming
Getting hotter by the hour
The animals are calling
Their homes now concrete towers

Factories going up
Forests falling down
When will Amazon?
Become another town

The trees have had their legs cut off
The animals scream for help
When will this stop they wonder
You hear a distant yelp

Splash! The sea's gone red
Smash! Other trees gone to bed
It will hit the floor so hard
The birds' nest is now dead

It is still possible
To change our nasty ways
Although I must warn you
It won't just be over in days.

Reece Smith (14)
London Academy, Edgware

The Youth Today

The youth are going to take over,
spreading apart the place all over,
What are we going to do?
They are spreading around like a virus.
These games that they are playing,
their parents are always paying.

They are taking over like an alien invasion,
They are supposed to be an amazing creation,
Look what they turned out to be?
Playing all these violent games,
Thinking that they can fly planes,
all they are doing is inflicting pain,
On those that are around them.

Soon society will be taken over,
Some of them coming home hungover,
They take anything that we are liking,
What happened to everyone cycling?

Rigon Osmani (14)
London Academy, Edgware

Cardboard Clouds

We live in a town,
Where up means down
And the void is always dark.

The lights overhead,
As we toss in our beds
Are waiting and watching above.

The shouts and the screams
Are simply our dreams
But no one remembers their name.

The secret police
Leave our minds at peace
As they march through houses and halls.

The cardboard clouds fall
On grass of child's scrawl
But where have the children gone?

And as the sun sets,
The people place bets
On who will last the night.

Lizzie Quinn (14)
North London Collegiate School, Edgware

'Twas A Rainy English Morning

'Twas a rainy English morning,
When I stood before the Thing.
Not many could guess, behind its faded whiteness,
The true message that could be read within.

'Come serve *your* country! Come serve *your* king!'
Was what the message appeared to say;
And I could only guess, how many doomed youth,
Would have signed up by the end of the day.

Harsh, bitter days and long, fearful nights,
That was all that lay ahead.
With each man soldier silently thinking,
By the end of the day, will I be dead?

For there is no glory, no honour, no courage,
Only bravery and a war that is hopeless,
An impending knowledge of Death,
A graveyard where you amongst the thousands rest.

So this is what I think, the message ought to say:
'Come to *your* doom. Come to *your* death'.
For once Death holds you in her silky grasp,
She will never let you get away.

'Twas a rainy English morning,
When so many men did die.
Each man lay bedraggled, on the bloody battleground,
With no one to hear his desperate last cry.

Savannah Harper (15)
North London Collegiate School, Edgware

What Are Friends For?

What are friends for?
Friends are there for caring, sharing and always there for listening

What are friends for?
Friends are to laugh with and have your heart filled with joy

What are friends for?
Friends are there to open your heart, open your mind

What are friends for?
Friends are there for times when you feel alone,
which is a feeling you will never get as long as you have a friend

What are friends for?
Friends are there through the night and day just for you

What are friends for?
Friends are there to give you advice when you need it

What are friends for?
Friends are there till the end

That's what friends are for.

Alastina Sinnathurai (13)
Park High School, Stanmore

A Child's Stolen Innocence

The scorching sun showers upon me,
Stretching its outstretched fingers,
Tapping me, bearing me in realisation
Who am I? What am I doing?
My chains of thoughts are disrupted,
By the echoing regulations
I feel the walls are closing upon me,
Like the ground is opening up, swallowing me in,
Drowning me into darkness and sorrow,
I look around managing to utter a phrase
'Help us'
My distant cries of agitation,
Are neglected by the camouflaging crew of children,
I'm also one, who's ignited with the fire of child labour,
Helpless, forlorn and lost,
But given away from an acceptable cost,
The family who I recall as my own,
Have discarded me, also known as being disowned,
Millions of us burden our ill fate,
I wonder, are we even God's kin
Or paying back for committing a previous sin?
Or is it what we actually believe,
The poor build-up of our so-called civilisation
We're treated unfairly,
And being paid low wages,
Paid less than an adult,
Because of our young ages,
Child labour is a crime,
And we have to save them from this misery,
And commit to making our future better,
Ensuring the past and present becomes nothing more than a mere history . . .

Kamelie Kandassami
Park High School, Stanmore

Valley Of Death

As I walk through the shadow of the valley of death,
I take a look at myself and realise there is nothing left,
And realise all the people I've left
And regret that fact they are all dead,
Now I have to pay their increasing debts,
When I have plenty of death threats,
I have one chance and I'm gonna bet,
On my brand spanking new television set,
Watching people smoking a marijuana cigarette,
Thinking they're gonna receive respect,
Streaming it live on the Internet,
To be honest you'd think I'm illiterate.

Yahya Omar (12)
Park High School, Stanmore

Guns, Guns

Guns shoot, we order,
As we cross the deserted border,
Enemies kneeling on their knees,
Begging for a life-saving plea,
We don't care and happily shoot,
In our proud and ridiculous suits.
Why do we cross the border?
Why do we shoot and order?

With guns you are not having fun,
When the job is done, the enemy is down.
Make sure you do it right for the fight,
When you see a gun make sure you run,
Don't delay make sure the job is done.
Have a beautiful life and have great *fun*!

Yousef Mereykhael (13)
Park High School, Stanmore

Change

Blood, blood, blood,
Everywhere I look,
Screams echoing,
Boom, a gunshot,
The shot fades away,
The sound of blood dripping onto the ground,
I want a change,
I live in a godforsaken wasteland,
Mankind is responsible,
They have caused turmoil,
I am now alone,
I wish for a change,
I hear cries of pain,
But I know I'm alone,
I want a change.

Dhirav Patel (12)
Park High School, Stanmore

Two Ends Of Law

Law, restraining me like handcuffs on a criminal,
Making me think I can't have my own say
Squeezing freedom out of me like squeezing flavour out of a tea bag, but why?
For my own good, for everyone's good, to show us what is right or wrong,
and to put criminals in their fit places,

Yet this tightrope of law is being stretched until it breaks, *snap*!
If this rope breaks it will be holding nothing but its own weight
Will both ends of the rope ever meet?
Who knows? Although it's in our hands.

Sabiha Rahemani (12)
Park High School, Stanmore

Evil Poverty

To the people who suffer,
To the children with no clean water,
Why is the world like this?
Why is there a difference between,
The rich and the poor?

How do you cope?
All I know is that you are you and I am not you,
I wish I could know how you feel?
I wander around thinking,
Of all the things happening in Syria,
Africa and Libya,
How do they live with evil at every corner?

Sometimes I wonder what life would be like,
If I were to be struck from my job
And put into poverty,
To the people who suffer,
To the children who have no clean water,
We feel your pain at every corner.

Rees Patel (13)
Park High School, Stanmore

The Holocaust

The lights never seemed to appear.
Only depression and fear
I stood there, staring at the sky.
Trying not to imagine what light would be like.
The sky seemed empty.
So was my heart.
I stood there behind the fences.
Trying hard not to cry.
I fell to my knees wondering what had happened to my parents.
A wind of happiness sprung into my head.
I saw my parents in the sky.
Calling me to come.
My eyes slowly shut whilst I felt my mother's arms around me.
My heart was not empty after all.
I was warm in my heart and never opened my eyes again.
God had let me free.

Aarabi Ganendiran (12)
Park High School, Stanmore

Global Warming

Beware, beware
As if you care.

The storm was quick,
But long to fix.

Moaning and groaning is not the answer,
Nor will it help the disaster.

Wake up now is the time,
Otherwise, tomorrow will be a climb.

Actions are all we need,
Or polar bears will be left to bleed.

In a blink of an eye everything can disappear.
But if we all care, there is no fear.

Harsha Daboo (12)
Park High School, Stanmore

Bang! Bang!

Another day gone,
another one lost.
Bang! Bang!

A mother's pain,
is the killer's gain.
Bang! bang!

The one who thought they won,
left the trail of blood.
Bang! Bang!

The youth of today,
Is the death of tomorrow.
The death of tomorrow,
killed the youth of today.
Bang! Bang!

This place is not the place to be,
where you love friends,
but cannot protect your family.
Bang . . .

Wait this cannot be true,
the gunshot's gone right through the chest,
I have killed a little girl,
but she is not at rest.
I go to run but the sirens call,
I look at the girl I am such a fool.
Bang! Bang!

Michael Sweeney-Slavin (13)
Park High School, Stanmore

Stormy Britain

As clouds open,
Tears of angels crash down,
Destroying the hidden beauty of the world.
Seas are raging,
Waves crashing against golden pearls,
Which glimmer no more.

The winds are whistling,
Mighty enough to bring down trees,
When will this weather end?
We plead.
Houses no more,
Underwater they are now,
Will help ever come?

The sun has gone to sleep,
The sun is no more,
When will the sun shine again?
Bringing us happiness and all.

Tegan Emery-Barker (12)
Park High School, Stanmore

The Rich, The Poor And The Passive

He eats from a golden platter served by his butlers;
She eats stolen bread with her brother, munched down rabidly
Someone shouts, 'Call the guards! The thief is getting away!'
Her brother gets taken and hung from a noose
There they stand, passive in the year 1514

500 years later and things barely changed
The rich still sit pretty and healthy,
While the poor skip their meals
The rich read resplendent, elegant books,
While the poor sit there, necessitous and penurious,

He gets what he wants, when he wants, and no responsibilities,
She drops out of school, no money to carry on,
He celebrates his birthday with a new set of car keys,
While she has to work double hours to feed her family,
Still, they stand, passive, in the year 2014.

Nikita Songra (12)
Park High School, Stanmore

Whenever I Hear Your Name

Whenever I hear your name,
I imagine nothing but total pain,
I imagine your voice trembling with fear,
The fear of dying any moment.

Your frail, fragile body was on the verge of collapse,
You never gave up, you never gave up,
Your courage to live overwhelmed those around you,
Although that wasn't enough to hold yourself forever.

Your warmth gave a leap of joy to everyone's hearts,
Your breathing made people weep till their eyes hurt,
Your children drowning in debt to you,
For them they were living because you existed.

My tears of sorrow are not enough,
Whenever I hear your name,
Although you are in Heaven,
You are always within my heart.

Nabeel Khan (13)
Park High School, Stanmore

Hidden In Shame

I was always the one,
Hidden in the crowd.
Nobody knew just
How I'd make it out.

Why I'd left . . .
Why I'd run . . .
Nobody can tell me now
That I was wrong
To say that it was long,
Since you held me.

Because I'll always be shamed and scarred now.
Hiding in the shadows
Just waiting for the night
Silently becoming the one
That lets out all the light

Why I'd left . . .
Why I'd run . . .
Nobody can tell me now
That I was wrong
To say that it was long,
Since you held me.

Yasmin Barud (12)
Park High School, Stanmore

What Kind Of Life?

No food to munch,
No clean water to quench,
What kind of life?

No place to learn,
No mates to hang with,
What kind of life?

Nowhere to eat,
Nowhere to sleep,
What kind of life?

No shoulder to cry on,
No one to rely on,
What kind of life?

What has the world come to,
Where children have no one to curl up to?
What kind of life?

How can they leave,
Us poor people to bleed?
What kind of life?

How would you like it,
If you weren't allowed to be excited,
And were left alone?
With this kind of life!

Aaliya Rehemtulla (13)
Park High School, Stanmore

Gaia

He did not care, that man,
When he cut down the last tree
On a stone-faced island far off in the sea;
He wanted only the wood, how selfish was he.

Neighbour killed neighbour,
When he felled that last tree,
Gull-bitten, bobbing, to Tartarus sank he -
Black blood-froth writhed shapes in the sea.

There's an ugly beauty in mankind, you see,
A logic and soundness in their insanity.
She saw his potential and nurtured him mildly
But he soon forsook Her pregnancy violently.

Crisp wood's for the fire, crisp wood's for the house,
Green rots to brown: Nature's children howl loud.
Their families are gone, their homes have burnt down
But he didn't care then and he doesn't care now.

Yet Gaia knows him and she knows us all well,
So think, on the day when you cut down Her tree
When you suffocate Her in tides of plasticine,
When you scorch Her, brand Her with coals and industry,

That mums can be harsh and Mother is Gaia
So when you claim innocence She'll know you're a liar.
Your dams will crumble, cities your filth mire,
She'll return you the favour: the sky will bleed fire.

Matthew Chalmers (16)
St John's School, Leatherhead

Alekhine's Gun

Looking over the amaranthine deep blue,
He felt like wax left unburned by a candle.
Fragments of dear Docteur Pangloss flicker -
'Tout est necessairement pour la meilleure fin.'

Perpetual hours spent; sweat congealing under the thighs.
Of course, what can't be taught by others must be learnt by self.
Resigned, legs apart, staring blankly. The contours on his
Neutral, weathered face illuminated by the unforgiving glare.

Blinded by deafening idolatry
A pious man thwarted by piety.
The real wolf hides not in the forest,
But under an esoteric red hood.

Searching for the right mask
To wear in the corner of that oak, nubilous haven.
The noise is insanity, the tick of the clock.
Her eyes were the most arrestive.

Pained, gaunt fingers stretch nonchalantly.
A heavy, hard, translucent tear forms.
The reassurance of the cool wood brings back
Memories of aubades read.

He always moves the queen last
A sagacious, albeit neoteric tactic.
The key to hallowed athanasia lies not on E1.

Ding!

Tom Fleming (17)
St John's School, Leatherhead

How Quickly Things Can Change

3-0 Ashes finished.
The proud three lions rejoicing,
The scared baggy greens retreating,
All frail and diminished.

21st of November Australia went to field,
England fail with the bat.
Mitchell Johnson improved his stats,
England's weakness was now revealed.

Jonathan Trott heads back,
Haddin works wonders in the tail,
The sweet story of the summer has just turned stale.
By the end of test 2 Mitchell Johnson deserves a plaque.

Soon Swann was to retire with immediate effect,
Kevin Pieterson began to cause unrest,
Australia were obviously blessed,
And now England's hopes were well and truly wrecked

5-0 Ashes over.
The proud baggy greens rejoicing,
The scared three lions retreating,
All frail and diminished.

Ed Hayter (14)
St John's School, Leatherhead

Mr Johnson-Jones

'Is a jaffa cake a cake or a biscuit?'
He poses the question.
In this regard the jaffa cake is a misfit
Does anyone have another suggestion.

'A definition of onomatopoeia anyone'
Yes, James Hughes
'The formation of a word from a sound associated with what is named, in my opinion'
Good answer, I respect your views

'Have you ever written on a banana?'
He asks.
This one has been grown in Ghana,
'Ok then, pass it around the class'

Tonight's prep,
To write a poem you say,
That's a tough homework you've set.
But I'll have to do it anyway.

Joshua Geddes (15)
St John's School, Leatherhead

Eagle

The white eagle rests on our breast pocket,
Watching; as our silent guardian.
Its mighty feathered wings flourished open,
Ready to aim at those things that are above.

The eagle will never leave us -
Sitting on its pearly throne.
Even when we are gone, and our rings have tarnished,
The watchful protector will always be by our side;
Resting on our breast pocket.

George Barrass (14)
St John's School, Leatherhead

Time

You spend it; you make it,
You buy it; you sell it,
You watch it; you miss it,
You wait for it, and pray for it,
But you can't control it

It can go fast or slow;
It can be kind or cruel;
It does not forget.
It's a second and forever

It's what people treasure most,
And offers chances to many.
It steals what means most to some,
Waiting not for who falls behind.

It cannot be created,
Nor can it be destroyed
But be warned
Its mercilessness stops for no one
Not for that or them or him or you.

Jade Simpkin (14)
St John's School, Leatherhead

Sleep

Drift off, plunge through eternal darkness,
Falling, falling, through the void,
Landing in Heaven; just how you like it . . .
Or Hell, just how you remember it.
Floating through old friends, happy memories and dream worlds,
Or engulfed by black humour playing on your mind,
All the scarring experiences returning to your fuzzy head . . .
Be careful, or your today may haunt your tomorrow,
Providing your yesterday hasn't already proved you dead.

Kyle Jackson (15)
St John's School, Leatherhead

Inspection Day

Once more unto the breach, my pupils, once more;
Or they'll close up the school for an academy.
Most weeks your teachers will settle for peaceful,
Modest attempts at learning.

But when the sound of inspection blows through our halls,
Then imitate the perfect, private-schooled pupil.
Arch the back.
Tuck the shirt in.
Disguise poor grammar with eloquent tones.
Listen politely, even in physics.

On, on you useless students,
Whose fathers, frankly, expected better.
I see you standing in the pews, straining upon the school bell.
Lessons are afoot; now, let us pray for England and St John's!

James Hughes (14)
St John's School, Leatherhead

Broken Rainbow Of Sin

Faded pride behind glazed magenta eyes.
Cyan, dissipating through fingers, staining veins with absent spirits.
Spattered electric green like envious freckles on cheeks.
Tears of freak orange dribble greed into the dry corners of the mouth.
Bittersweet lemon yellow merely drenched the hair, soaked in anger.
Lips; crimson and lustful, sought desire yet dripping with regret.
Scattered too easily across her body is
A broken rainbow of sin.

Jordan Cox (14)
St John's School, Leatherhead

THE MODERN MONSTER

Can we talk?
No, sorry, no time to talk, I will text you later,
Strange? Nobody has time to talk anymore.

Each of us has been infected with the disease,
Twitter, Facebook, Instagram, Tumblr,
Friend requests rather than friendship,
Gaining followers is all that matters.

Likes on this, likes on that,
Type out what I think and see if it gets some hits,
What to post? When and where?
Does anybody read it? Does anybody care?

Children as young as nine,
Always seem to be online,
Shouldn't they be riding on their bikes,
Instead of pressing 'like'.

It's real life written as ones and zeros,
It's messing with my head,
Is the art of conversation really and truly dead?

Shaliya Patel (14)
St John's School, Leatherhead

The Unwanted Journey

I get the train every morning
You could say it's rather boring
Eagerly at the platform waiting for a glimpse
The freezing cold which really shows the wimps
My train comes in at 7:54
No standing in the cold anymore
The long red train finally shows
The awaiting passengers, about to blow
You suddenly catch the sight of an empty seat
Your warming heart skips a beat
You charge and throw yourself towards it
It's suddenly taken, the selfish twit
As the houses whizz on past
I stand here with my face against the glass
As the train approaches Leatherhead
You find yourself thinking, 'I wish I was in bed'
Catching the train is hardly a perk
But it is quite useful for poetry homework.

Hannah Chantler (14)
St John's School, Leatherhead

Fine

F ighting an internal war invisible from the outside
I n your struggle, forever alone
N eeding to scream to be heard above the deafening silence
E veryone believing the lie. I am fine.

Josie Davies (17)
St John's School, Leatherhead

War

It starts with an argument.
The tradition began long ago.
It seeks not to be a malevolent force.
Nor does it take sides.

But we have shaped it,
lovingly crafted it,
and bent it to our will.

Human nature demands it.

We have tended to it,
added fire to the flames,
over the millennia.

It only grows worse,
the destruction and death,
when we fuel it with weapons,
created to bring pain and suffering.

To us it's a game.
To outwit the enemy.
A grand strategy.

Which nobody wins.

There will come a day,
when we douse it,
with a petrol so full of hate,
that it will burn brighter than ever.

And then it will be too late,
and the world will burn,
in the fire we lit,
all those years ago.

Jack Perry (14)
St John's School, Leatherhead

The Time Of Cricket

Now new faces arrive in dangerous Australia
I've watched England linger with failure
Had old players feel unworthy
The new players feel hunky dorey

Time spent watching Aaron Finch get a ton
Of which stops Cooky's fun
My my at the MCG Aussie rule is here to stay
Life-long dreams broken, England want to run away

And at SCG Morgan's here to fight
I've never hoped more that the Poms just might . . .
Never in a million years. Damn Faulkner staying in like that
Felt like I've seen such a Pratt

This is a horror, 9 in a row for Australia
Before we offer the devil a prayer!

Never can we win the fourth ODI
Felt like why? Oh why?
This will start me crying
Way too far when Kylie says your team is bad
Before I could deal with it but a man goes truly mad

Now 2014 24th January 11:32
I wish my spidey senses awakened. I detect a breakthrough
Swear like mad Geddes in maths with giddy delivery
It says that we have achieved victory

The beautiful morning
Truth is told when I say what a beautiful day
And the sun is finally dawning
I know it is Parfait

Owe it all to you?

Alastair Fleming (15)
St John's School, Leatherhead

You Are

You are like a soundless lion,
Hunting for his prey,
You are like a shiny sharp silver knife,
Waiting for its next victim,
You are the old crumbling down graveyard,
Slowly watching the people die,
You are like a green sprout,
That no one will ever like,
You are the deep dark black hole,
That every person is afraid of,
You are the big tower block,
Powerful yet so weak.

Sebastian Zablocki (14)
St Mark's Catholic School, Hounslow

Fear

Fear's face is a pale dull white.
His hair long thin shreds of thread.
He wears a coat of sorrow and shame.
He drowns people with horrific worries.
His teeth made of shattered glass.
His breath is filled with evil ghosts.
He sleeps in the depth of a stomach crowed with torturous thoughts
He dreams of neurotic images.
His children are shivers down your spine.
His ambition is to shadow people with torments.
His enemies are joy.
He craves on depression.
And hungers on disturbing memories.

Tom Stitson (14)
St Mark's Catholic School, Hounslow

The Tree Poem

In the summer, I wear a green fur coat that covers my body,
and changes colour during autumn.

In autumn, my green fur coat transforms into a sunset-orange colour,
and I gently pick off my coat very slowly.

Winter has come and I am a naked being with no coat,
and I am shivering through the harsh, violent snowstorm.

It is still winter, and I have frostbites all over me and I am still waiting for spring to come;
but I remember the joyful moments when it was summer,
I can see the birds resting upon my long, brown branches singing a peaceful melody, through my ears . . .

Spring has come and the harsh, frostbiting, shivering winter has passed away,
and my bright green coat slowly crawls back to my body,
ready to generate warmth and comfort towards my body.

In thunderstorms, hear the loud, crashing bangs and the fierce,
fast, striking lightning and that paralyses my whole body in a shock.
This is the worst time of the day. With lots of heavy, splashing rain coming down,
like meteorites from the sky and brutally splashing down to the ground.

Summer has come back, and the bright, shining sun has reached the top of the sky,
radiating the warmth to every living being. All the harsh moments have finally gone,
but this is just another start to a harsh new journey . . .

Axl Santos (14)
St Mark's Catholic School, Hounslow

You Are

You are bleakness of black, gloomy and cold making all light absent.
You are the bitter winter, peaceful and still unclothing the naked trees.
You are the isolated night, abandoned and lost for words.
You are the sinister Venus flytrap, brutal and effective, having no mercy on its victim.
You are the roaring floods, filling up with anger and leaving hearts broken.

Osaze Urhoghide (13)
St Mark's Catholic School, Hounslow

You

On a day I was unable to control
Fate decided to take its toll
It showed me the face of an angel
A flawless spirit
An escort through my existence

I, a powerless juvenile
In my delicate core
A little light
Was to ignite

Many memories with you were to be made
Gradually being buried
As time went on
You were a home
An infinite love

The astute words were absent
From my naive mind
So you filled my head
With knowledge to assist me
Through the incomprehensible complications
That I would have to contend with
In my later years to come

As time swiftly went on
Disability took over
Although your fire from within kept burning
your flame began to flicker
And your days began to burn out
Soon I knew that you would be gone

Sorrowing
You became a candle
My night light by my bed
To keep me unharmed
As I lay and rest my head

And now as I continue my expedition
You are by my side
Not plainly
But in my heart and mind.

Eleni Yiasouma (14)
St Mark's Catholic School, Hounslow

Dead Inside

There once was a boy.
He walked alone, dragging his feet.
Nobody was by his side;
Nobody was there to envelop him in comforting arms.
His bleak face revealed no emotion,
Except despair.
Grief.
Agony.

His eyes were of the deepest black,
Blacker than his ragged clothes.
And in their ominous depths hid a wasted soul,
That started out unseeingly,
Hopelessly,
Like a vulnerable child abandoned by a deserted road.
But his eyes were filled with something sadistic -
Echoes of a haunting past,
Memories that imprison in their clawing, merciless clutches.

Nightmares.

Each night this boy would lie in bed,
While shadows slithered around his mind,
Their frigid breath delicately tickling his ear.
Murmurs.
Whispers.
Shrieks.
The serpents would twine around his neck,
Silencing his broken screams.

He was senseless.
Forgotten.
Numb.
He was not alive;
He was dead inside.

And so this boy walked alone, dragging his feet,
His only dreams of rotten hearts and piercing screams.

Klaudia Zaporowska (14)
St Mark's Catholic School, Hounslow

Fear

Fear's face is laughing,
But inside he's angry.
His sharp red nose as hard as rock,
But his hard black eyes stare,
Drowning you with fear.

His sharp yellow teeth,
Sink into the hearts
Of tormented children,
Through tales of dread and horror.

He creeps along the creaking floorboards of your mind.
His slick, black hair curls up at the ends,
Like his lips that curl into a smile,
Whenever he hears a child scream.

Rose Stephens (14)
St Mark's Catholic School, Hounslow

Fear

Fear has a face of your most feared creature,
His messed up hair is dyed with red.
He only wears a death-scented perfume,
And its rotten smell can be smelt miles away.
His teeth are made from red-hot flint,
His breath is filled with the scent of blood.
He sleeps in the darkest depth under your bed
But when you look
It will be the *end!*

Anderson Speck Randam (14)
St Mark's Catholic School, Hounslow

You Are, Poem

You are the piercing deadly red lava escaping from volcanoes.
You are the perishing frostbite that seizes on victims,
during freezing harsh winters.
You are the freezing cold bitter winter nights,
that send shivers down my spine.
You are the Venus flytrap that awaits its prey and pounces,
like a cat on a ball of string.
You are the scorching blazing hot core of the earth that is sizzling,
like sausages in a frying pan.
You are the furious rhino charging at its innocent victim.
You are the dark deadly moment war was announced on the radio.
You are the dark beastly vile feeling of death as it comes calling,
to another innocent soul.

Mikey O'Shea (13)
St Mark's Catholic School, Hounslow

You Are

You are a crystal clear blue.
You are the sun brightly shining in the summer.
You are the fabulous sound of the bell at the end of the day that brings joy to my day.
You are the flower that everyone loves, the red rose.
You are the sun that brings light into me.
You are the puppy dog that shows love and affection.
You are the bright and intelligent computer that has all the answers.
You are a beautiful island separate from all the normal places.
You are a guitar which plays happy music and makes people happy.
You are a strawberry Ribena nice and sweet
You are . . .
A wonderful mum.

Tom Sloan (13)
St Mark's Catholic School, Hounslow

You Are

You are a weak and old weasel,
Cowardly hiding from your most
Dangerous enemies.
You are a dreadful poison ivy bush,
Anyone that comes near you
Is instantly maimed
You are as black as space,
Sucking all oxygen from
People's lungs.
You are a cold butcher's cleaver
You break bones and
Tear meat like you are
a vicious dog.
You are like a dreadful bully,
Breaking down everyone's courage
And thinking you are better
Than them.
You are like a cold-hearted murderer,
You do things intentionally
And don't look back or regret what you have
Done.

Cameron Randhawa (14)
St Mark's Catholic School, Hounslow

Joy

The face of joy shines full of light.
His hair is made out of colourful locks of rainbows.
His teeth shine bright like the sun.
He wears a shirt of beautiful nature.
His enemy is evil.
He wants to give love and happiness to the world.
He lives in a colourful house of amazement.
His dreams are making everyone happy the next day.

Darren Snarski (14)
St Mark's Catholic School, Hounslow

Depression

Depression's face is the face of the Devil.
His eyes are the eyes of the families left behind, a path to the empty soul.
There is no longer a hair on his head, for it's now just a distant memory.
Depression wears nothing more than an old ragged robe.
Depression's job is to haunt more innocent people every. Single. Day.
To slowly kill people.
Turning innocent souls into haters of themselves.
Blackening the hearts of lovers.
He rips the blanket that's keeping you warm, leaving you half naked in the icy snow.
He wears an empty smile on a blank face.
His hair made from knives that he uses to constantly stab naive people,
His guilty pleasure.

Depression shall die.

Alex Whiddett (14)
St Mark's Catholic School, Hounslow

Depression

He wears grey ripped up rags.
His eyes are always closed.
His head is grey and bald.
The only sound he makes is him moaning.
He is unloved and alone.
His dreams are full of loneliness.
His breath has no smell and no taste.
He sits in the shadows and corners of dark rooms,
Alone.

Samuel Taylor (13)
St Mark's Catholic School, Hounslow

You Are . . .

You are an advanced computer.
Brainy and intelligent, answering
Any challenging question.
You are the balmy days of autumn.
Lovely at day but ferociously cold at night.
Leaves dropping every minute.
You are the redness of a burning fire.
Blazing and steaming destroying wood
Into ash.
You are a beautiful poppy.
Exquisite and graceful whistling
In the wind.
You are the fresh gum in a packet.
Minty and icy white, awaiting
Your time to be.

Stachel Tumwa (14)
St Mark's Catholic School, Hounslow

Guilt

Guilt's face is a picture of painful memories.
His hair is a dishevelled mess from the sleepless nights.
He wears a robe of dark rags, an invisible weight crushing sloping shoulders.
At every waking moment, self-accusation brutally attacks his conscience.
His teeth are glass, crunching and shattering with every lifeless moan.
His dreams are screams of dying children.
His eyes, neurotic as they scan the street, slinking into the darkness.
His pulse the speed of a hornet's beating wing.
His conscience an overpowering leader, possessing his every thought.

Anna McConnell (13)
St Mark's Catholic School, Hounslow

Despair

Despair's face is a picture of gloom.
Her eyes are full of hopelessness but she still feeds on yours.
Her smile is wretched and meaningless yet
She creeps behind people's minds waiting to attack them
She battles with joy, happiness and hope.
She engulfs us, overpowering our emotions.
She feeds on your grief until she gets bored of you.
She laughs at us in the dark when we suffer through dark times.
For she is despair.

Natalia Rola (13)
St Mark's Catholic School, Hounslow

Love You Too Much

To leave you below
I'm coming back to you
Just like I promised
I'll soothe the fire
Tend the wounds
Just like when you were five
And you fell from that tree
Dad told you to walk it off
But I kissed it
Stopped your crying
I do it again now
With the hole in your heart
Give me a year
And I'll be there
Underground
Back to you.

Abi Pelham (15)
The Angmering School, Littlehampton

Brown Twigs

Dark emaciated twigs crippling at the ground,
being dusted with dirt and grit from the land,
no nutrients can feed these brittle, withered branches,
left in the mud to soak dry in relinquishment.

Parched of the sap given naturally by the tree,
it could not be spread through the tips,
to reach the bedded fingers crackling their boned knuckles,
for the luxurious touch of receiving their portion of sustenance,
but they never grasp it.

They have no appearance as they blend in to be one,
a crowd of frail carcasses carved out harshly,
by the eroding of bitter winds and seasons of pain.
Their face is a mask of bones.

They are left to rot at the grunge of the ground,
where the gloom is at its thickest,
no ribbons of sunlight can grasp the cloudy floor,
so it becomes cold in its drought.

Higher up in the safe breeze of the wind,
the nourished pale branches of the tree are blessed with blossoms,
they have no ability to look down as their greedy necks,
are addicted to the sun,
they neglect the dead and dying beneath them.

Safe and secure from the ground,
with their minds too leafy to apprehend,
but down in the soil drying up into twigs,
there are the bodies, of the distant malnourished tree.

All the agony of hunger and damage heats the twigs in this draught;
they spark their last breath to the doors of awakening death,
flickering a flame of anger to burn down the tree.
Letting the bark melt unpleasantly to the floor,
as the last blossoming petal turns to ash,
crumbling into dust to sink to the bottom joining the twigs to be equalised.

The tree had to be burnt to begin.

Natalia Boothby (14)
The Angmering School, Littlehampton

I Don't Want To Die Either

Shoot me
Go on shoot me
Ride the bullet into my chest,
and keep on spinning until you
fall from dizziness,
no?
I'm not your enemy
Your friend
Not your best friend
Probably not close enough to be invited,
to your funeral
But I'm your last friend
This is an empty world
You and I must live to share
Can you do that?
No?
Then do it
Pull the trigger
Let your fingers loose,
get them comfy
Make the squeeze
It's for a better cause
You won't save the world
I doubt you'll change it
But it's just us now
Here it is real
Realise it,
then pull out your gun
Feel the weight in your sweating palm,
have you ever shot it?
No?
It's just like paintball
Except you can aim for my aching head
I won't mind
It doesn't even hurt
The numbness fades
Like us in time
Maybe if we survive this
You and I can go,
paintballing

We can become best of friends
And you can regret killing me
Shaking,
and waging a war against me
The crimes you've committed
Remember them
But don't tell them
It will be just like a birthday party
From your broken childhood
Where you wished upon those candles,
no?
Maybe you should host one
in your dusty soldier uniform
I'd bring you a present
Chocolate or something else from,
a sale from the shop around the corner
Now
To watch you smile
One last time
I'd be there because
Here it's just you and me
Together yet alone,
and that gun facing me
You're my world
I love you
I love you
Hold me
Make me in your image
Like a sculptor
Sculpting cold ice
So we can melt down,
together
But first
We will die
Together
Together
Go ahead and kill me,
no?
There's nothing to lose
Not a penny

Money doesn't matter to me
It doesn't matter,
because here it's just us,
and I cannot buy you action figures,
or try at the shooting gallery to win,
a goldfish
Nor can I buy you a soft tissue
To dry your,
crying eyes
But I, no you,
yes
You
Know I will die the same,
no
We,
yes
It's inevitable
Running around in circles
Until the end of time
We will die the same
We will die, so
Please don't kill me
Please
I don't want to die,
either.

Harry Dilks (17)
The Angmering School, Littlehampton

Teddy Bear

She was innocent
He was lifeless

She wore pigtails,
Ringlets of golden waves
Plaited by tender fingers

He was a big softie,
Coated with auburn fur
From head to toe

Wherever she went,
He would follow

Salty tears from her emerald eyes
Little droplets on his fur,
Like dew suspended on grass
On a frosty morning

Held in her arms,
He brought her delight,
A smile to her face
Like a husband does a wife

The innocence came and went,
Dark shadows crept into her light
As the sun set early
Summer love turning into winter fright

She grew up
He stayed still

Her eyes were open
Seeing suffering, feeling pain
Whilst his remained unblinking,
Still innocent,
Still safe.

Sophie McCluskey (16)
The Angmering School, Littlehampton

The Angel Maker

Hush now
Stop your crying
You're not dying
You're simply flying free
I've raised you up
Depart from your shelter
Of earth and meat
And send your prayers to me
I've raised you up
Disband my fears
And wipe my tears
Send forth my final plea
I've raised you up
Take the skin from your back
To expose the crack
You hide internally
I've raised you up
Create your wings
From human things
Your blood is not your fee
I've raised you up
Your breath is wrought
Your time is short
You must go peacefully
I've raised you up
Suspended your bodies
The harlequin copies
Of the angels you could be.

Francesca Finch (15)
The Angmering School, Littlehampton

Mirrors Lie

Mirrors lie to us teenagers, looking back is a complete stranger.

The numbers on the scales take us over,
Measurements rule us, society's cruel,
And the numbers tell us who's who.

Our faces are blank canvases, fresh and bare.
We primp, prune and style our hair.
Foundation and blusher, concealer and mascara, hide behind the mask.

Skinny jeans, tight tees, whatever will be next?
Crop tops and shorts, what about 'skorts'?
The fashion is never the same;
If it isn't short or showing your bum, then you're considered lame.

Society teaches us to hate ourselves;
We're made up of the products on the shelves.
Fake tan, hairspray, I don't care what they say, you're not skinny, pretty or thin.

Smoking weed, having sex, whatever will be next?
Countless diets, horrendous riots, we're getting ourselves a bad name.
Drink this! Try this! The pressure's all too much.
Don't and you're on your own, you won't fit in that much.

Sweaty and dim, running for thin, you must never give in.
Society's wrong, life will go on, you've been beautiful all along.

Demi Sadler (15)
The Hope Service, Epsom

Recovery

She scratched her head and sighed to herself.
She couldn't take her eyes off her old friends on the shelf.

She smiled and laughed much stronger than before;
she turned off the light,
shut the door.

Her razor-kissed wrists were beginning to fade;
her favourite song on the radio played.

So proud of herself, she started to smile.
She hadn't harmed herself in a while.

She was so much better again,
but the feeling came every now and then . . .

She opened the door, turned on the light.
She picked up her razors and said goodnight.

With her arms full up, she chucked them away.

Today was a new day.

Saffy
The Hope Service, Epsom

Natural World

We create as we destroy,
Great cities, for all to enjoy
We get told, others behold
What mysteries are shown to unfold

We haven't cherished what we have changed
What nature intended to keep the same
We won't see nature's final masterpiece
What will she have to unleash?

Emily Bromley-Ellis (14)
The Weald School, Billingshurst

Apocalypse

All that's left is infinite darkness,
Deep black is all that's left now,
An eternal life of surviving,
Is there really point anymore?
The unbreakable pattern of inevitable gloominess is killing life itself,
Since the world is decaying, what's the point in trying?
Is fighting for life worse than putting an end to it?
Since the world is taking its last breath,
Maybe I should take mine,
The skull of death haunts my mind every night,
Sleep is unimaginable,
How life used to be is becoming a blur,
I can't even remember the reassuring sound of my mother's voice,
The only joy left is where her soul lays in Heaven,
And that's where I'm going too.

Laura Kershaw (14)
The Weald School, Billingshurst

The Floods

Rain comes flooding in
Through the kitchen door,
New and old furnishings throw in the bin,
Water splashing on the floor.

Wind's whistling through the windowpane
There's a duck paddling in my bedroom.
The garden's flooded, what a shame
I hope I can play out there soon.

The government are having an argument
But there's no money left
I hope the arguments are not in parliament
And we don't want any theft.

Somerset has been hit badly.
I can't help this situation.
We can't stop this rain, sadly
Our troubles are all across the nation.

Verity Pearce (14)
The Weald School, Billingshurst

Home

As the sun comes up over the shabby town I call home,
my ears adjust to the noise of trucks chugging, men muttering.
My eyes are left squirming with the Indian sun,
as I arise from the hard, dusty ground, that is my bed.
It's not as it seems, this place I call home,
but I try to stay strong for the sake of the young,
in the hope that one day, their lives may be fun.

I stumble through the hustle and bustle of the morning rush,
the foul-smelling odour that lives in my nose,
follows me around and sticks to my clothes.
I keep my brother and sister close as that is all I've got,
our bare feet clambering as we head for our daily scurrage.
Rubbish and bottles and any spare food,
water from the river that doesn't do us any good.
I wish I could go to school.

At 6 o'clock as the sun goes down,
we trudge back home to our street corner,
to reveal our finds, we see what we can sell,
bottle caps, wrappers, a couple of torn-up clothes,
I guess we will be sleeping and starving again tonight.

Milly Tucker (14)
The Weald School, Billingshurst

Tiger

He walks unseen, a beast of stealth and cunning.
He follows his prey to a stream where it's running.
But tigers can swim so time is up
And for the mouse that was running, it's all bad luck.
But we are the tiger and the tiger are prey, so think of the tiger and save one today.

Emma Clemens (14)
The Weald School, Billingshurst

Round And Round The Mulberry Bush

Early swim in the gravel
Resting your head in the wild
Journeying the tunnel from A to B
Bouncing on the wooden frame
Weekday hikes
A hole in the hedge
Chalk sprinting down the road
Tiny wheels going back and forth
Collecting the monkeys
The solid glass
Growing in a messy, cramped space
Disorientation upon return
Never sleep despite the name
Squeaks when you get home.

James Holcombe (14)
The Weald School, Billingshurst

The Youth Of Today

Young in their face but old in their minds
Their choice of words deceive whose inside
Walking with heads low but hoodies held high
The youth of today all wear the disguise

Not a nice one, it's one people despise
For they walk the street at night shadowed by lies
Never do they they walk alone, usually groups of guys
Like a plague, people avoid them or so do they try

However there is a lighter side for dark is only half
The youth of today who strive and succeed
At those I do not laugh, I would like to hope I am one of them
As then I'm on the right path, the path to success will cause some distress
However in the end we'll be some of the best.

Josh World (14)
The Weald School, Billingshurst

The Rhino

Feet thudding,
Tears running,
Lungs wheezing,
Blood rushing.

Blurry-eyed,
And laced with fear.
Straining ears,
He sheds a tear.

Guns blazing,
Voice squawking,
Eyes darting,
Life squandering.

Gunshots,
And loud cries.
Not a trace of angst,
Between their lies.

A fallen hero,
A life once loved,
A wasted casualty,
Among the hubbub.

Trees whistling,
Ground shaking,
Wind hissing,
Rain crashing.

No more is the fallen angel,
Left alone chasing stars.
He takes bow,
He takes a breath,
For the rhino is sat on death's doorstep.

Isabelle Lofts (13)
The Weald School, Billingshurst

Like Bullying To A Child

A growing woodland, like peers to a pupil.
A standing difference.
A single spark, like a knife to a killer.
No evidence
A carving in the centre, like tearing to a letter.
A expanding forest.
Flowing fear, like blood to a casualty.
Repetition.
Feasting fear, like diseases to a brain.
Repetition.
Sparks ignite into flame, like problems to a panicker.
Trees; the fuel.
Every cell clouded by smoke, like water to a drowner.
Every oak sided.
A sudden loss, like death to a survivor.

Katie Chapman (13)
The Weald School, Billingshurst

Sleep

Yesterday you were in a mood,
And at first I thought you were being *rude!*
But then I remembered your sister had just been born,
So you might be a bit ripped and torn,
It was all in my head,
You just wanted to go to bed,
Tell me if I'm wrong,
But I am quite proud of this little song,
I know I am not good at rhyme,
But I hope you get better in time.

Rose Moran (13)
The Weald School, Billingshurst

Drowned In Poverty

Drowned in poverty, this broken town lies to waste
Nothing but dust lies in this space.
Drowned in poverty, this poor boy left to die,
He has no one here to wish his goodbyes.

We are wealthy living in peace
We have no worries to what we must eat
Yet we still complain about the minorities in life
Our words, so bitter, we cause such strife.

The pain, the anguish, all of which we don't feel,
But we feel it for them, the ones who appeal,
When they are on our screens we feel their pain,
But what do we do? Nothing, but who shall we blame?

Drowned in poverty, we watch as they survive
Whilst we live on, healthily, as we strive.
Drowned in poverty, they are living in threat
Whilst we sit back to try and remember to forget.

Jake Snelling (13)
The Weald School, Billingshurst

Deserted

The silenced land
Where life is banned
The lakes abandoned, the rest just sand

The death zone
Danger prone
The land scattered with flesh and bone

The smell of death
Not a single breath
Once a thriving world, easy to forget

What is to come
Of this colossal slum?
No hope of a future, this world is done.

Joe Tucker (13)
The Weald School, Billingshurst

Change In Times

I have painted pictures,
for all of my life,
paintings of street scenes,
and everyday life.
I have painted the famous,
the infamous.
I have painted all,
the world's fickleness.

My first was landscape,
a sunset at the beach,
and birds on the horizon though,
no people did breach,
the sense of tranquillity,
created by each,
movement of oil on a plain canvas.

The next was a hill scene,
of tough terrain,
drowned in sorrows,
made wet by the rain.
It told of times gone by,
when nothing was in vain,
and all had purpose and meaningfulness.

My last was a women,
and pretty was she,
but her nightlife adventures,
she had to plea,
if not they'd be laid bare,
for her Mr to see.
Sitting in her element,
another man's arms.

I painted the revolution,
the change in our race,
a race where everyone's drowning,
in the ocean of grace.
I don't have the time to maintain these regrets,
I just see a society full of old threats.
The old makes the new,
and the new makes the next.
Tangled in a hex.

Samuel King (14)
The Weald School, Billingshurst

Caged

What is this thing we're locked in?
What is this thing we're mocked in?
What is this thing that seems to be,
Forever between you and me?

What is this thing we're kept in?
What is this thing we're left in?
What is this thing that's always been,
Dividing me and my twin?

What is this thing we're bed in?
What is this thing we're fed in?
What is this thing that's always stunning,
At how it stops us from running?

At last I have the answer,
To the question we all know.
This thing that always traps us, mocks us, keeps us,
Is my friend a cage.
This final answer gives a question,
For now we need to know,
Who is this thing that keeps us here?
And will they let us go?

Isobel Sherlock-Fuidge (14)
The Weald School, Billingshurst

Sticks And Stones

I hide my battered heart away
Wrapped in plaster, signed by myself
I don't want to hurt anymore

The sticks and stones,
they broke my bones
But the words will always hurt me

Thc timid little victim in me had cried out
'Why?' to her tormenter
I was answered with crueller punishments for whatever I did

They'll forget me in a few years,
go on with their lives while I can't stop living in the cold past
You'd think for all the pain they cause me they'll at least remember my name?

Or perhaps they'll stay as they are,
troubled, cold-hearted bully, no longer fun to be around
No friends left

Future me will approach,
with a smile on my face
'Congratulations you are all alone.'

Megan Cork (14)
The Weald School, Billingshurst

My Mother Is No More

3.6 tonnes of life crashes to the floor
My mother is no more
Poachers rub their hands with glee
I turn my back and flee
For my mother is no more
I stomp through the savannah but I know I'd rather
Be stomping with my mother
But my mother is no more
I see zebras cutting through the plains
But they cannot cut through the chains
Which bind her to her deathbed
For my mother is no more
I loved to feel her gentle spray
Teaching me how to play
And showing me the way
Of life
Something she no longer has
Because my mother is no more
Now my mother's just decaying fat and bone
Her tusks a part of a dictator's throne
My mother is no more
Now here I stand at the watering hole
Trying to fix my broken soul
Because my mother is no more
And it's tearing me apart!

Morgan Walmisley-Davies (13)
The Weald School, Billingshurst

The Words Of The Loved

Sometimes people are beautiful
Not for the way their hair shines
Their lips pout
Their eyes glisten
Sometimes people are beautiful
For the words they think
The words they know
The words they share

Sometimes people are ugly
Not for the way they hurt
The way that they judge
The way that they break
Sometimes people are ugly
For the words they think
The words they know
The words they share

And sometimes words can soothe the
Dark cracks in the mind
The holes in the soul
The tears on the cheek
And that is how they felt
As she reminded him
Of how the sunlight
Felt on his skin
And he reminded her
That she was
Alive.

Sophie Tapson (14)
The Weald School, Billingshurst

The Forest Morning

The frost crystals glint and shine early in the morning,
The animals slowly rise moaning, groaning and yawning,
The holly berries sparkle; hanging daintily from the trees,
The eyes that watch, follow the tiny busy bees.
Whistles of wind and crunch of leaves,
As the scampering badger thieves.

The animals run and ears prick up as they are prey,
They all get away, apart from the squirrel, who is led astray,
Hope he comes back soon not gone all day,
Also hope he isn't just a body in decay.
Soon they worry, running to look,
And they find him,
Dead by the brook.

Oscar Hart (14)
The Weald School, Billingshurst

Endangered Animals

Why are these animals coming to death?
But as I scream I hold my breath,
Animals dying every day,
And all of them dying in one way.

They are getting killed for their fur and tusks,
Fur for decoration, tusks for medicine,
It's not them dying for a reason,
It's us hunting them down.

This is not needed,
This can be stopped,
But it is still getting done a lot,

These animals don't have to suffer,
But why do we always kill their mother?
Save these animals from extinction,

Because they're not dying for a reason.

Jordan Smith (12)
West Derby School, Liverpool

The Homeless

All alone in the night
With hardly any clothes
Scared of the light

He sleeps by the bin
Without a care
No friends to be seen anywhere

His family has vanished
Left him alone
He was left without a home

He goes to sleep late at night
Curled up in a sack
Scared of getting a fright in the night.

Jack Kenwright (11)
West Derby School, Liverpool

The Man

The man roams,
like a stray cat, thinking,
where the next meal will come from . . .
Is it fair that a man roams the streets?
A bin is as full as a buffet to some . . .
A half-eaten chicken leg, a companion to some.
Is it fair that a man roams the streets?
A stranger to friend or foe,
the man is a desperate shadow,
stuck in a eternal void,
never to show his face again.

Owen Caveney (11)
West Derby School, Liverpool

Back Then And Now

During my childhood,
where I used to play.
There was a place,
where I used to stay.
It was full of life!
When the birds used to sing.
Then the forest springs used to refresh the souls of us all.
I walk down the path and look around,
And then sniff the air,
that makes me feel safe and sound.
The forest trees give me shade,
from the sun that hits me like a blade.
Now when I walk there, there is no more sun.
No more friendships that made us one
The buildings are grey,
And *Rome* the town.
Buildings that make me feel depressed and finally down.

Gift Anegbode (12)
West Derby School, Liverpool

Lycaon Pictus

Lying in the African sun,
The wild dog's work was finally done,
After hunting all day and night,
The spotted dog's were now out of sight,
Lycaon Pictus is now under attack,
But WWF needs your help to fight back.

The endangered animals are all alone,
Left by themselves, without any home,
They fight for survival,
Waiting for your arrival.

The African desert is now very plain,
Leaving all the animals in and out of pain.

Stephen Spence (12)
West Derby School, Liverpool

The Homeless Man

As night comes I search for food and shelter, somewhere to rest my head,
somewhere to call my bed.

I hold in my hand a plastic bag with nothing but clothes and my country's flag.

I put my head in the ground in search for something I already found,
was it my pride or was it my freedom? Buried in the ground I search for a reason.

I've told you my story, I tell you no lie, I have to go it's about to end,
I have a terrible pain in my eye.

Bailey Gillies (11)
West Derby School, Liverpool

Lonely People

Walking the streets by the bins always thinking nobody wins all alone.
No friends nothing to do whilst other people are driving Mercedes-Benz.
Thinking will there ever be a day when I'm rich,
memorising how this started, no way he thinks.

Junior Kasauubu (11)
West Derby School, Liverpool

Volcano

They wake, they rumble, they roar, they blow, they look, they pour,
the hot pouring magma comes down on the town, they scream, they flee,
but the magma is too fast . . . They scream, they shout, they whimper,
they fall silent, and the ash makes them slowly fade away.
Until there is only a thick layer of ash.

Aaron Reynolds-Worrall (11)
West Derby School, Liverpool

End Of The World

The end is coming
The meteors start forming
The buildings burn
My stomach churns
I watch people die
I start to cry.

Blood is screaming down the street
I watch as it soaks my feet
I don't know were my family are
I can't see the car.

I start to moan
My stomach groans
The buildings fall I start to scream
I wake up crying
Thank God, it was just a dream.

Kyle Howey (12)
West Derby School, Liverpool

The Falcon

They begin to descend into the dark abyss,
all it can see is a big blur,
except for its prey, right over there.
As it braces for impact, its claws appear ready to strike,
it will cause pure fear.
Its flight is dead on sight and it's in the zone,
blink you've missed it in a flash,
its prey is dead and he has got his trophy.

Adam Madden (11)
West Derby School, Liverpool

Who Knows What The Future Holds

We live to look for one thing
To find one thing
To search for one thing
That thing is unknown
We live to choose one thing
To decide one thing
To select one thing
That thing is unknown
We live to love someone
To care for someone
To be happy with someone
Who that may be is unknown
We live for a reason
For a point
For something
We live to achieve our goals
To reach our potential
Because it matters not what someone is born but what they grow to be
For who knows what the future holds.

Daniel Burns
West Derby School, Liverpool

Danger, Danger

Save our animals. If we have no animals the world wouldn't be the same.
Crash, the last shark jumps and crashes on the surface of the water.
Crash, the last elephant crashes into a tree. Boom, the last tiger roars.
Rainforests destroyed, seas empty, no animals to be seen,
deserts empty and dry with no life.

Josh O'Connor (12)
West Derby School, Liverpool

War

Across no-man's-land the guns roar,
And in the sky the shells soar,
That strike down soldiers far and wide,
That make people want to hide,
They fight because they have to.

Soldiers die every day,
But they know it is the only way,
While citizens wait anxiously in their homes,
They fight because they need to.

All those soldiers who died in pain,
Do not let their dreams be in vain,
For as they ascend to the sky,
On the battlefield their bodies lie,
They fought because they wanted to.

Thomas Logue (12)
West Derby School, Liverpool

The Storm

Lightning strikes, thunder roars, wind bellows and crows caw.
This is what it's like on the day of the storm.

The rain smashes down with a terrible bang then rolls down the windows without a sound.
Children whimper, cry and call, this is what it's like on the day of the storm.

The city is busy, the centre thrives and the clouds roll across the sky.
Now people hide away, hoping for another day.
This is what it's like on the day of the storm.

No one is left but rubble and dust and all the cars are nothing but rust.
This is what it's like on the day of the storm.

Adam Day (11)
West Derby School, Liverpool

World War

All around me I see destruction.
Bombs falling like the wounded.
Bombers' engines roaring in the sky.
As I look I am staring Hell in the eyes
With its fire behind it.
As I see fear I shed a tear.

A black hole is my heart as I have lost my friends.
In my trench I fear the worst the whistle sounds,
I climb my ladder over the top of my trench, the German guns blow.

Thomas Durkin (12)
West Derby School, Liverpool

Tsunamis

A giant wave came,
it was horrible and threatening.
It washed away everything,
trees, rocks, animals and people.
No one survived.
The island had sunk.

Steven Huang (11)
West Derby School, Liverpool

Whose Fault?

The forests are all gone, cut down by who?
The animals' habitats are gone, no home to go to.

The seas and oceans have no fish,
harpooned and caught, served on a plate.
Who is doing this, whose fault?

Whose fault is this, why would anyone do it?
Killing endangered animals even making them extinct,
It is our fault.

Joe Carroll (11)
West Derby School, Liverpool

Typhoon Haiyan

Swooshes, smacks, crashes and more.
Screaming louder than a lion's roar.
Showing no mercy to woman or man.
The mass of destruction that was Haiyan.

Ripping and raging trees like toys.
No mums and dads for girls and boys.
Buildings and houses knocked with ease.
No prayers or pleadings would make it appease.
It plunged the area into dismay
Some took from shops without thought to pay.
Poisonous gases spewed into the air.
Homelessness, hunger, hostility, despair.
More than six million people were displaced.
The worst natural disaster that has been faced.
So lying in bed, cosy, full and warm.
Why not spare a thought for the victims of the typhoon storm?

Sam Mullally (11)
West Derby School, Liverpool

Tornado

It is twisting through the air like a mouth of death
Eating its way through the ground and trees
Violently destroying the world and ruining lives too
Nothing breaks its path and it is queen bee sending its bees
Scarier than a ghost, more frightening than boo
This is a tornado

Sucks everything in its body, never anything left
Faster than lightning, cyclones look at their wrath
Leaving towns empty and cities bereft
The destruction of it is bad, nothing is alive from its path
This is a tornado

Tornadoes are fast powerful disasters
They have no mercy for human beings
When it dies it's a happy time
But it will rise again and no one will be fleeing.

Thomas Murray (11)
West Derby School, Liverpool

The Beautiful Game

The beautiful game goes round and round,
in the world cup final only one winner is crowned,
The beautiful game has evolved quite a bit,
putting on that jersey and walking out in that kit,
From Diego Maradona and Zinadine Zidane,
Not many people can do what they can,
Now to the modern-day heroes like Ronaldo,
With all the players travelling to and fro,
Although the game is not perfect with the fans shouting out,
When the players are starting their hearts fill with doubt,
With ninety minutes up but the game is not done,
all of the clubs with enough money to buy the moon and the sun,
With the abuse we hope to be gone,
The players think it's over, but the game still lives on.

Callum Bandell-Childs (11)
West Derby School, Liverpool

The Bear

The almighty bear emerged from his cave.
Looked to the sky for a new day.
Clambered down the mountain on which is his home.
The bear went hunting only to find a bone.
He searched some more with bated breathe.
But only found that every creature left.
He then saw there were many missing trees.
But that wasn't all in the human killing spree.
He went to the river with great upset and great thirst.
But only to find a thing far worse.
The water had been drained and a large dam instead.
The bear thought that soon he'd be dead.
The bear wandered home to find a mound of rubble that was his cave home.
He realised that he would be alone.
The bear was fearful that he was next, he heard a sound behind his fallen nest.
A number of hunters wielding guns, they pulled the trigger and so another creature goes.

Elliott Cullen (11)
West Derby School, Liverpool

Bang!

My name is Dan,
I am 19 years old,
My friends are funny,
They all think I'm bold,
Jack my friend has an idea,
Let's go pay those idiots a visit,
I start to fear,
They give me a gun,
I feel so powerful,
But this is no fun,
I approach a gang,
All alone but with a weapon,
Bang! Bang! Bang!
I look down at my stained top,
Covered with blood,
I come to a stop.
My name is Dan,
I'm 19 years old,
My mother is crying,
Over my grave so cold.

Nathan Dubber (11)
West Derby School, Liverpool

Zinedine Zidane

Zinedine Zidane, remembered as a great one
But it only took one head butt and like a flash he was gone
The Champions League came by
And that volley made the fans cry
The ball curled in the air like a baby's frizzy hair
The 2006 World Cup final rolled around
And Materazzi hit the ground
Zidane frowned and Italy were never crowned
With a cloud of shame to his name
He retired from the world game.

Jamie Marsden (12)
West Derby School, Liverpool

Remembering The Soldiers

Remember the soldiers that saved our lives,
Remember the soldiers that took our hearts.
Remember them today.

Remember the soldiers that sacrificed their lives
While we watched the time fly by.
Remember the soldiers.

Remember the soldiers that fought night and day,
Remember the soldiers that got struck down.
Remember them today.

Remember the soldiers that took our breath away,
Remember the soldiers that flew away.
Remember the soldiers today.

Remember the soldiers that died for us,
Remember the soldiers now they're gone.
Remember them today.

Stephen Mills (11)
West Derby School, Liverpool

Election Day

This big topic is highly based on the government's list,
Day by day checking, trying to fool the public with words of mist.
Taking opportunities is important in this game,
Trying not to fall on their own sword and trying to escape the pain.

The decisions they make apparently are very important,
The opposition are ready to pounce as they lie dormant.
The public take a big part in the events to come,
After this ugly affair leaders will want their mum.

When the day comes leaders turn into generals,
Trying to beat the other party, charging over them all like animals,
The battles will be fought by the ballot box, where public have their say,
The lives of these people decided on Election Day.

Jack Moorcroft (12)
West Derby School, Liverpool

Godzilla!

It's a normal day in Tokyo.
Everyone is shaking from head to toe.
It's Godzilla loose again,
but look! Here come the army men!
It's a rivalry dating back to '54,
when Godzilla first knocked on Tokyo's door.
However, to him, tanks are just toys.
Then, the general shouted, 'Run, boys!'
He breathed fire hotter than a stove.
Away all the cars drove.
Godzilla roared - couldn't be beat!
However, his foes come on the street.
Ghidorah, Gigan, MechaGozilla too.
Then, Godzilla called the crew!
Anguiras! Rodan! Mothra! But that's not all!
Baragon and Varan were also standing tall!
They looked each other in the eye, the scene was set!
It was by now their fists had met!
Godzilla went in, all guns ablaze!
You could tell this epic battle was going to go on for days!
However, the enemies had little allies,
until SpaceGodzilla came from the skies!
Megalon came up from the ground,
but then Godzilla took him to the pound!
Mothra took care of MechaGodzilla.
This battle was really a thriller!
Rodan and Anguirus took care of Gigan,
but by now the aliens had all run.
The battle was over; all you could hear were cheers!
You could tell Godzilla had changed over the years . . .

Will Robinson-Cooke (12)
West Derby School, Liverpool

Bomb Squad

Dust in his eyes, sweat trickling down his face and the sun protected from his eyes,
by the sandy coloured helmet he wore on his head . . .

His team had his back. He heard a click, *don't move,* he thought.
His team slowly, cautiously walked over, fully loaded, aiming at the high grass.

Then they sprang like rabbits being bolted by ferrets.
The bad guys. The enemy. They spread rounds in a 180 degree turn,
killing him and his team.
Tick.
Tick.
Boom!

Kieran Jennion (12)
West Derby School, Liverpool

The Phone Number

Society and how it's obsessed with flappy birds.
Fantastic
Long-lasting
Amazing
Purely annoying
Proudly dumb
Yes it is bad
Broke phone
Infuriating
Raging
Dead bird
Stupid.

Ben Cawley (12)
West Derby School, Liverpool

Liverpool FC

From Shankly to Brendan we followed our team,
Rome to Istanbul we've followed our dream,
Our journey is long, but dream stays the same,
To keep for our children, the famous red name.

Wherever we are, wherever we stay,
Be sure the kopites will seize the day.

Forth is our destiny, our passion and pride,
Liverpool football club,
The world's greatest side.

Bobby Turner
West Derby School, Liverpool

Lightning And Thunder

Lightning flashing way up high,
while the thunder booms in the gloomy sky.
Thunder strikes and brings the earth,
to its end.
Lightning flashes and blinds the eyes of the world.
The thunder sounds like everybody in the world,
is clapping simultaneously.

Rhys McCarthy
West Derby School, Liverpool

Hot But Sweet

Volcano, volcano you're so hot!
I really admired you rushing down my road burning everything in your path,
but I love it, because it's true and you look so like caramel.
So I want to lick you,
but if I did I would go to ash straight away
So children, don't go by a hot volcano, otherwise you will turn to cinders.

Ethan Canty (11)
West Derby School, Liverpool

War

Bang! Bang! Here and there,
guns going off everywhere!
It's like an explosion in my brain . . .

Shoot the enemy twice again.
A lonely soldier in Afghanistan,
trying to stay alive the best he can.
At the RAF base the coffin stands draped, in the Union Jack.

A sign that life just didn't come back.
A mother's son lies cold and alone, so brave.
A hero! Now he's home.

Owen Conroy (12)
West Derby School, Liverpool

YOUNG WRITERS INFORMATION

We hope you have enjoyed reading this book - and that you will continue to enjoy it in the coming years.

If you like reading and writing poetry drop us a line, or give us a call, and we'll send you a free information pack.

Alternatively if you would like to order further copies of this book or any of our other titles, then please give us a call or log onto our website at www.youngwriters.co.uk

Young Writers Information
Remus House
Coltsfoot Drive
Peterborough
PE2 9BF
(01733) 890066